THE
Star Tales
OF MOTHER GOOSE

For Truth
Mary Stewart Adams

For Beauty
Patricia DeLisa

For Goodness

Copyright © 2021 by Indigo Star, LLC
All world rights reserved.

No part of this book may be reproduced, stored in a retrieval system,
or transmitted in any form or by any means electronic, mechanical, photocopying,
recording or otherwise, without the prior consent of the publisher.

ISBN 978 1 7364120 0 8
Contributing Editor Jennifer Carroll
Published in partnership with Mission Point Press, Traverse City, Michigan
Printed in the United States of America by Walsworth in Marceline, Missouri

THE
Star Tales
OF MOTHER GOOSE

For those who seek the secret language of the stars

Mary Stewart Adams

By Mary Stewart Adams
Illustrated by Patricia DeLisa

Patricia DeLisa

Indigo Star, LLC.

When we are children, we look to the sky with wonder, our imagination ready for story and adventure. But too often the opportunity is lost—light pollution erases much of the beauty we might see, and no one is there to teach us the stars. Here is where *The Star Tales of Mother Goose* shines. With clear prose and colorful illustrations, this book offers every child—and the child in us all—a chance to learn the night sky. And once learned, this knowledge becomes part of us forever.

I first met Mary Adams by phone a decade ago when I was writing *The End of Night*. I was down in North Carolina and Mary up in northern Michigan, but her excitement about night skies made the distance disappear. I heard a voice made for telling stories—exuberant, passionate. In the years since then, I've been lucky enough—on the "dark-sky coast" along Lake Michigan, and in Duluth—to see Mary in action. She is a storyteller who draws you in—you can't not be excited about the stars. With *The Star Tales of Mother Goose,* she matches her words with Patricia DeLisa's colorful art and brings that excitement to the page.

The truth is, it's only through the efforts of people like Mary that we will re-connect with the night. Most of us—if we live in a city, certainly, or a suburb, most likely—live swamped in artificial light. If we're under the age of forty, we have probably never lived where we can see the Milky Way. Our overuse and misuse of artificial light at night—which we often refer to as "light pollution"—has grown steadily over the past decades. When I was a child in the early 1970s, living west of Minneapolis, we could still see the Milky Way overhead. But that view of the heavens has long since been erased. Most Americans have no idea what a real night sky looks like, what a view they're missing. It's up to people like Mary to invite us to remember and to learn about the amazing sights overhead.

~Paul Bogard, author
The End of Night

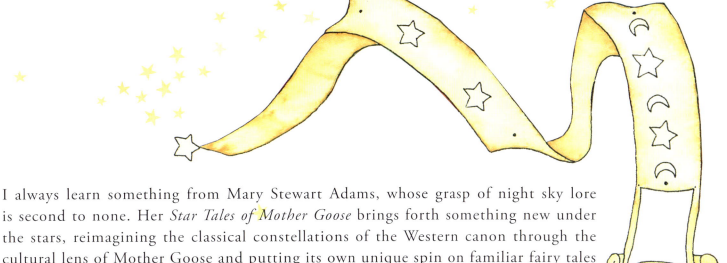

I always learn something from Mary Stewart Adams, whose grasp of night sky lore is second to none. Her *Star Tales of Mother Goose* brings forth something new under the stars, reimagining the classical constellations of the Western canon through the cultural lens of Mother Goose and putting its own unique spin on familiar fairy tales and nursery rhymes. Vividly illustrated with her sister's fanciful art, this book evokes the wonder of childhood when it seems that anything is possible, and reading it makes me want to go outside tonight and reacquaint myself with old friends—the stars. A must-read for anyone ready to approach the night sky anew with the wide-open eyes of a child, whether they have kids of their own or are simply kids at heart.

> John Barentine, Ph.D.
> Director of Public Policy
> *Internation Dark Sky Association*

Mary Adams has found delightful celestial meanings in the classic nursery rhymes. For instance, "Sing a Song of Six Pence" is on one level a description of the elaborate French culinary creations called entremets. But its King could also be the constellation of king Cepheus, near the top of the celestial sphere; his Queen is Cassiopeia; his counting house is the Milky Way, the treasure he counts is its myriad stars; the honey comes from the Beehive cluster; the maid is Virgo, hanging out the laundry on the clothesline of the ecliptic; and the four-and-twenty blackbirds are the hours. And other details—such as Hydra and the Northern Crown—ingeniously fit. This beautifully illustrated book is like a splash of enhanced color on the mosaic of the sky.

> ~Guy Ottewell, author astronomer
> *Universal Workshop, Astronomical Calendar, To Know the Stars*

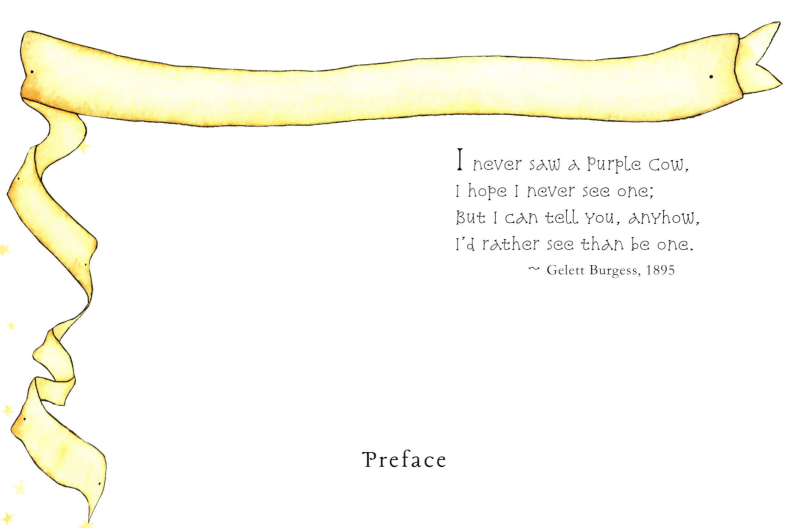

I never saw a Purple Cow,
I hope I never see one;
But I can tell you, anyhow,
I'd rather see than be one.
~ Gelett Burgess, 1895

Preface

The ideas found here were inspired by an encounter I had with my five-year-old niece when I was in my early 40s. The result of this encounter has been the growing awareness that there are few things as delightful as finding your way through the stars than by way of a nursery rhyme. Though we usually leave such ditties behind when we emerge from the kingdom of childhood, this book is designed to stir that whimsy again, to lower the drawbridge over the moat we crossed into adulthood, and to restore the avenues of access to that which inspires joy and wonder in relation to the celestial world around us.

I was visiting my sister, and my niece was gaily singing a little ditty I had never heard before: "I never saw a purple cow, I hope I never see one, but I can tell you anyhow, I'd rather see than be one." Always one for a rhyme that tickles, I asked her where she learned it, and her reply was, "Mother Goose." What was significant in this moment was that I considered myself very well-versed in Mother Goose, and the fact that such a delightful rhyme should have escaped me must mean that it wasn't a true Mother Goose rhyme. What did my niece know?

Much to my chagrin, my sister produced her copy of *The Original Mother Goose*, the very edition I had grown up with, and flipping to the appropriate page, she proved to me my ignorance and my arrogance. There it was, Gelett Burgess' ditty from the 1890s smiling up at me from the page.

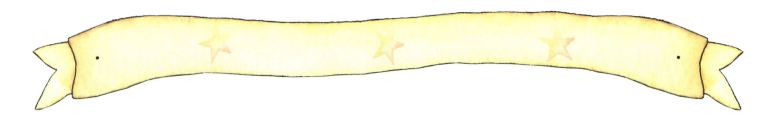

I was crushed, and I confess, I went to bed angry that night. I am the seventh of eight children in my family, and there are few arenas in which I can really prove myself beyond my siblings—at least I had Mother Goose. But not now. As I pulled back the bedsheets, I was angry that I had missed that rhyme; as I fluffed the pillows I had to grapple with the reality that I didn't know Mother Goose as well as I thought; and as I lay awake most of the night, I wrestled with the fact that I had been undone by my five-year-old niece, on my very own turf. This wasn't just a little ditty, this was the stuff of my identity, deeply rooted in how I approached my parenting, my work, my whole way of being in the world.

And then something mysterious and wonderful happened.

As the Sun rose the next morning and its first rays slanted toward me where I had finally fallen asleep, I received a message, "Mother Goose is Cygnus. Mother Goose is Cygnus," over and over again, until I slowly woke up and realized what was being whispered to me. It wasn't just that Mother Goose is the constellation Cygnus, but that the rhythm and whimsy and joy in language is a gift from the stars. I knew that the ancients believed that the starry regions were populated by divine beings, and that these beings sent their forces through the zodiac to grant form to the human being's physical body, but did that include the gift of speech? Well, yes! And not just any speech, but rhythmic rhyming riddling delightful witty speech, like Mother Goose. All at once, the constellation Cygnus the swan, formerly fixed with majesty along the Milky Way river of stars, became animated in my mind's eye, every flap of her wings beating out a rhythm that made its way earthward as a delightfully bouncing rhyme.

I was stunned, for I realized in that moment that I had developed a flat plane of consciousness with regard to the stars, considering only the 12 regions of the zodiac in relation to the human being, and not the other regions beyond the zodiacal plane—and there are 76 of them! All at once I found myself in multidimensional space for the very first time, lifted beyond the singular plane and into wholeness.

And so this book, *The Star Tales of Mother Goose,* which is my attempt with my sister to share the joy of living in relationship with the stars through whimsy and rhyme and once upon a time.

It must be noted here at the outset that the point of this book is not to immediately unveil the mystery of the connection between nursery rhymes and the stars for the children in our lives. It is, rather, to let this knowing sink into our own thoughts, to nourish our own imaginations, so that when we approach the night sky with a child, we will be sensitive to the need for sustaining awe and wonder as long as possible, rather than calling on the intellect too soon. It is the hurry to know that can flatten the plane, as it were, deflating the wonder that is so needed in our thoughts about the world.

Weight, measure, and number are sound elements in the physical realm, while joy and whimsy fleet by, inviting us to look beyond, into the mystery of once upon a time. Gleaning inspiration from the words of Bulwer-Lytton's title character Zanoni, *The Star Tales of Mother Goose* takes as its foundation the idea that, "There are times in life when from the imagination, and not from reason, should inspiration come." Taking inspiration from the imagination rather than reason is not an activity confined to childhood, it is, rather, a gift from the stars, available to the human being any time and every time we are faced with challenge or crisis, whether personally or globally. Sing-song and happily-ever-after have an almost magical quality of restoring one's sense of truth, goodness, and beauty in the world. This was the goal of the *trivium*, also known as the Liberal Arts of Language, which sprang up in the Middle Ages, when the nursery rhymes included here first began to appear.

Further, such an approach to the world around us asks us to be like the stars themselves in the lives of those in our care: to shine, but not to diminish the sacred dark through which we shine. It is oftentimes in the dark where imaginations have their tender beginnings, and what we find in the process is, just as we seek to know the stars, so, too, do they seek to know themselves in us.

Mary Stewart Adams

Contents

Part I
Traditional Rhymes of Mother Goose

HOW TO USE THIS BOOK
xii

SING A SONG OF SIXPENCE
5

THE LION AND THE UNICORN
8

HEY DIDDLE DIDDLE
10

LITTLE BO PEEP
12

LITTLE BOY BLUE
14

HUMPTY DUMPTY
16

MOTHER GOOSE
18

OLD KING COLE
20

BANBURY CROSS
22

GOOSEY GOOSEY GANDER
24

Interlude

MOTHER GOOSE HISTORY
27

Part II
Star Verses by Mary Stewart Adams
With History, Guides & Maps

SING A SONG OF SIXPENCE
40

THE LION AND THE UNICORN
44

HEY DIDDLE DIDDLE
48

LITTLE BO PEEP
52

LITTLE BOY BLUE
56

HUMPTY DUMPTY
60

MOTHER GOOSE
66

OLD KING COLE
70

BANBURY CROSS
74

GOOSEY GOOSEY GANDER
78

Part III References

GLOSSARY
84

NAMES AND PLACES
90

BIBLIOGRAPHY
95

QUICK AND HANDY PAGE GUIDE
96

How To Use This Book

*A guide for understanding how we settled Mother Goose
and her stars into their places on the following pages*

There are four main sections to this book:

Part I

The first part includes ten traditional Mother Goose nursery rhymes whimsically illustrated by Patricia DeLisa. In this section, we devote two pages to each rhyme, with illustration of the main characters and key elements. Small star maps accompany each ditty, to hint at what's coming at the end of the book—where all happily ever afters belong.

Interlude

Between Parts I and II you will find an historical account of the course Mother Goose has taken through the ages, pieced together out of the clues she left along the way, from the moral imaginations of fairy tales to the delightful play of nursery rhymes.

Part II

Part II begins with a verse by Mary Stewart Adams that links the traditional rhymes of Mother Goose in Part I to the stars overhead in the night sky. Following the verse is a brief history of when and where the traditional rhymes first appeared, and how Mary, as star lore historian, has imagined their connection to the stars.

The next two pages in Part II provide a star seeker's guide and a map of the night sky, enhanced with Patricia's characters for ease of identification, and to tickle the funny bone. Once you've been introduced to the rhymes and their starry counterparts, the maps will provide essential guidance around the night sky. To get the correct orientation with the map, face north and hold it over your head. Also note that the constellation names on each map are written with all capital letters, whereas the names of individual stars begin with a capital letter followed by lower case, according to best astronomical practice.

Part III

To enhance your journey through the stars with Mother Goose, we've provided a few handy references: a glossary of astronomical terms; a list of pertinent people, places and heroes; our bibliography of secret sources; and a quick guide for finding the rhymes with their corresponding maps.

Part I

TRADITIONAL MOTHER GOOSE RHYMES

CHARACTER ILLUSTRATIONS

SMALL STAR MAPS

Interlude

A HISTORY OF MOTHER GOOSE

Part II

STAR LORE HISTORIAN'S VERSE

HISTORY OF TRADITIONAL RHYMES

GUIDE TO FINDING THE STARS IN THE SKY

STAR MAPS, INCLUDING CHARACTERS FROM THE RHYMES

Part III

REFERENCES

 These little boxes will come in handy for finding your way from the rhymes in Part I to the maps in Part II. You'll find them in the bottom right corner of matching pages.

The Star Tales of Mother Goose

Part I

Traditional Rhymes of Mother Goose

There

was a time when the stars spoke to human beings, and though they have grown silent now, this silencing didn't happen all at once, or even entirely. Through long ages there have always been those who could hear and understand this speaking, and who could read the starry script, while the others, they slept, and sleeping, they could only dream.

These star readers have been known by different names through every age, secret names that were hidden so as to not expose the sacred knowledge they bore.

Perhaps most hidden among these storytellers of the stars is

the Mother Goose

and her tales may go something like this....

SING A SONG OF SIXPENCE
TRADITIONAL RHYME

Sing a song of sixpence
   a pocketful of rye,
Four and twenty blackbirds
   baked in a pie,
when the pie was opened
   the birds began to sing~
Wasn't that a dainty dish
   to set before the king?
The king was in the counting
   house, counting all his money,
the queen was in the parlor
   eating bread and honey,
the maid was in the garden
   hanging out the clothes,
when along came a blackbird
   and tweaked off her nose!

April Night Sky

CORONA BOREALIS
The Crown

LEO
The Lion

MONOCEROS
The Unicorn

The lion and the unicorn
were fighting for the crown,
the lion beat the unicorn
all around the town.
Some gave them white bread,
some gave them brown;
And some gave
them plum cake
and drummed
them out
of town.

HEY DIDDLE DIDDLE

Hey Diddle Diddle
The cat and the fiddle
The cow jumped over the Moon,
the little dog laughed
to see such a sport...

...and the dish ran away with the spoon.

MAP 51

11

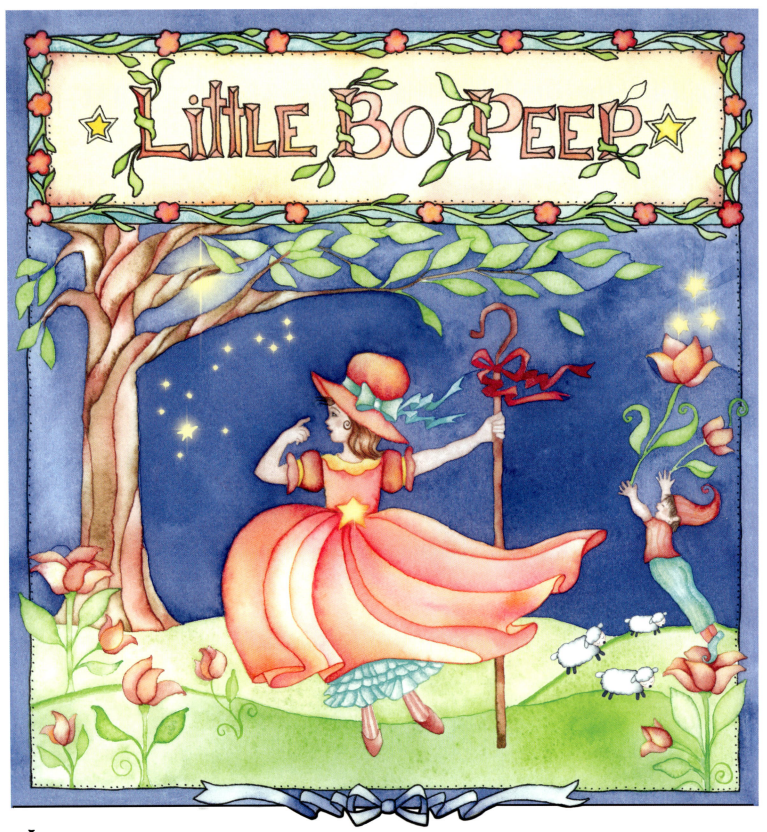

Little Bo Peep has lost her sheep and can't tell where to find them.
Leave them alone, and they'll come home,
wagging their tails behind them. Little Bo Peep
fell fast asleep, and dreamt she heard them bleating;

But when she awoke, she found it a joke,
for they still were all fleeting.
Then up she took her little crook, Determin'd for to find them;
she found them indeed, but it made her heart bleed,
for they'd left all their tails behind them.

Little Boy Blue

Oh why does the boy stay so fast asleep when his dear friend needs help with her wandering sheep?

May Night Sky

Little Boy Blue, come blow your horn,
The sheep's in the meadow, the cow's in the corn.
But where is the boy who looks after the sheep?
He's under a haystack fast asleep.
Will you wake him?
No not I,
For if I do he's sure to cry.

MAP
59

Humpty Dumpty

Humpty Dumpty sat on a wall,
Humpty Dumpty
   had a great fall.
All the king's horses
   and all the king's men
couldn't put Humpty
   together again!

Old Mother Goose when she wanted to wander would fly through the air on a very fine gander.

October Night Sky

CEPHEUS
The Old King

Old King Cole was a merry old soul, and a merry old soul was he, He called for his pipe, and he called for his bowl, and he called for his fiddlers three.

MAP 73

And a very fine Fidddle had he

Banbury Cross

Ride a cock horse
to Banbury Cross,
to see a fine lady
upon a white horse,
with rings on her fingers
and bells on her toes,
she shall have music
wherever she goes.

Goosey Goosey Gander
whither dost thou wander?
Upstairs and downstairs
in my lady's chamber.
There I met an old man
who wouldn't say his prayers,
I took him by the left leg
and threw him down the stairs!

The Star Tales of Mother Goose

Interlude

Once Upon a Time...

In contemporary culture, Mother Goose is usually depicted as an old maid in a bonnet, spinning nonsense rhymes to amuse babes while she sweeps the cobwebs out of the sky. But this is just one aspect of a deep and rich history that reaches back in time through many cultures until it arrives in the pre-Christian era of Perchta, a pagan goddess from the Upper German regions of the Alps that seems to have been an amalgamation of Germanic and Celtic traditions.

Her name, Bertha in English, may mean "the bright one," or "hidden one," and with her cousin Holda, she shared an interchangeable quality of sometimes appearing beautiful and white as snow, or elderly and haggard. Perchta and Holda shared the role of guardian of the beasts and appeared during the 12 Holy Nights of Christmas, overseeing the spinning. They were also connected to the miracle of animals gaining the power of speech on Christmas night.

To be a Mother Goose in the lineage of Perchta was to be one who was initiated into the ancient knowledge of the human being's origin among the stars and to have progressed so far in deepening and experiencing this knowledge that all things revealed their names, even those things of other, starry worlds. In esoteric circles, the one who had achieved this level of knowing was referred to as the "Swan Initiate," and her stars were those of Cygnus, the celestial swan that sweeps along the Milky Way, prophesying light for the universe with each beat of her mighty wings. Once the mysteries of the world revealed their names to them, the Swan Initiates no longer bore their own names. Instead, they were given titles that veiled their true identities, titles that were understood by those rich enough with imagination to understand. Such initiates wove tales of inner delight inspired by the greater harmony of the cosmos that had been revealed to them, tales that always began with "once upon a time" and came to joyful conclusion after the hero exhibited the same moral wisdom exhibited by the Swan Initiates. The Swan Initiates wove this wisdom so seamlessly through their tales that the dragon of fear, doubt, and denial would not know where to strike, so all things resolve in their happily ever after.

As a would-be Swan Initiate, the Mother Goose also stands in a long line of the divine feminine keepers of the star knowledge, dating at least as far back as the Ancient Egyptian Temple Complex of Dendera (c. 2250 BC), where, in a chapel dedicated to Osiris, there was carved in the ceiling

Temple of Dendera

In the Ancient Greek sky maps of Ptolemy (c. 90-168 AD), the divine maiden Virgo was no longer depicted as standing upright near the Lion as she had been by the Egyptians, but as reclining, as though she would fall asleep along the ecliptic. The ecliptic is the path followed by Sun, Moon, and planets as they seem to wend their way through the cosmos.

Eventually, Atlas turned to stone, and this divine feminine was as though slain by the world of reason and logic that gradually overtook the living imaginations of the ancients. And while the Cherubims and a flaming sword were set to guard the gate that is East of Eden in the Genesis story, a dragon was set as guardian over the world of living imaginations of this divine feminine being. To awaken this imaginative consciousness is to risk arousing this dragon—and so there is whimsy and rhyme and once upon a time.

a bas-relief zodiac depicting four women standing as the pillars that uphold the starry heaven. In the heaven can be seen the stars of the maiden Virgo, upright near the Lion, a crown of stars at her head. Advancing through the ages to the Ancient Greek culture, we find that in the place of these four female pillars of the heaven is the Titan God Atlas, who had taken the heavenly world on his own mighty shoulders, while his daughters, the Hesperides, guarded the sacred tree that bore the golden fruit. In a foreshadow of what was to come, Atlas gave these pillars of the heavens to Hercules to bear for a moment, an indication that the ancients believed there would be an eventual descent of the sacred star knowledge from the celestial realm, to be borne fully by the human being out of his own striving, without the might or guidance of the divine beings of a prior age.

Historically, the first person to bear the title of the Mother Goose may have been Bertrada (Bertha) of Laon, born in the 8th century in the north of France. She was known as the queen with the goose foot, and she was, most notably, the mother of Charlemagne. Legend holds that through

the inspiration of her father, Charibert de Laon, Bertrada nourished a high moral wisdom in Charlemagne through fairy tale imaginations, as only a Swan Initiate could. Her goose or "club" foot lent itself to this legend, because it was believed that the goose-footed were a link between the earthly and the spiritual worlds—as though they had one foot in each and could tell the tales of one to the other—the same way the swan, as envoy of a higher power, can both swim and fly, bound neither to watery nor airy worlds. The tales she shared with her son were informed by these other worlds and recounted how both seen and unseen forces work in human destiny, and, as a result, in history.

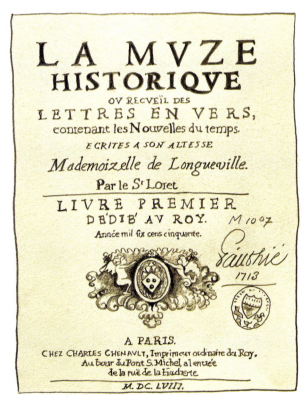

After Bertrada, nearly 900 years passed before the first written reference to Mother Goose appeared, in four lines of rhyming verse penned by Jean Loret (1600-1665), publisher of a weekly "gazette burlesque" called *La Muse Historique* in Louis XIV's France. Loret, sometimes regarded as the father of journalism, composed his epistles about society and artistic life in verses written in the form of letters to a friend. His reference to Mother Goose (La Mère L'Oye) in 1650 suggests that the term was still widely understood long after Bertrada the goose-footed queen, which is a testament to the enduring role of the Swan Initiates through the ages. By the time of Loret's written reference, the Swan Initiates had been sacredly and anonymously tending to the moral wisdom hidden in the true names of things for centuries, carefully sustaining the living imaginations streaming from the greater, cosmic harmony, and sharing this abroad as fairy tale wisdom.

While Loret is regarded as the father of journalism, it was his contemporary Charles Perrault (1628-1703) who laid the foundation for the literary genre we know as the fairy tale and who identified

"Out with you upon the wild waves, Children of the king. Henceforth your cries shall be with the flocks of birds."

its source as the moral imaginations of the Mother Goose. Perrault was a member of the Académie Française and he consulted with Louis XIV on his famous labyrinth maze of hedges in the gardens at Versailles, suggesting to his royal highness that the groups of sculptures and fountains depict Aesop's Fables. The water spraying in jets from one fountain to the next was meant to represent the speaking of the creatures to one another, a gift traditionally bestowed by the Goddess Perchta.

After he retired from royal service to the Sun King in 1678, Perrault published his *Tales From the Past with Morals—The Tales of Mother Goose* the first written collection of fairy tales from which we get such timeless tales as Cinderella, Little Red Riding Hood, Puss in Boots, Sleeping Beauty, Bluebeard. Prior to this period in the late 17th century, these *Tales of Mother Goose* were part of an oral tradition that was shared only by word-of-mouth, as was required by the sacred source from which the tales sprang. Charles Perrault's role in the unfolding destiny of Mother Goose was to bear the risk of writing the tales down, to gather them like fallen stars and organize them on the page. He was not the Mother Goose, but the scribe of that sacred storyteller.

It is also worth noting that it was not happenstance that it took 900 years from the time of Bertrada of Laon for the title of Mother Goose to appear in print, and there are countless fairy tale examples that reveal the wisdom rooted in this cycle of time.

The legend of "The Children of Lir" in the Irish mythological cycle is such a one. In the tale, the beautiful children of the king are turned into swans by an evil stepmother: "Out with you upon the wild waves, Children of the King! Henceforth your cries shall be with the flocks of birds." She curses them so that they must wander three mighty bodies of water for 900 years before the tolling of Christian church bells will break the spell and they will be freed.

Such a tale inspires a significant picture to come to life in the soul, and points to the mystery that to be transformed into a swan, to lose one's name and identity, was code for achieving initiation of the third degree, the so-called Swan Initiation. This meant the individual was no longer bound to this world, nor to the other, but was instead freed to serve everywhere as the inspiration for understanding how the mighty impulses that weave cultures together are unbroken through long ages of time, rising up in history and then

seeming to disappear. During the time of their seeming disappearance, these impulses are not lost, they are instead nourishing the soul of a people from within as moral imaginations, to take wing according to their own rhythm when the time is ripe. These imaginations appear as the lore and tales and ditties and fables that are shared by candlelight, at bedsides and in imaginations about the divine and sometimes mischievous beings that populate the natural world around us. To become the tales of Mother Goose they must endure the ravages of time and emerge intact, bearing their wisdom on the swan's wings of once upon a time into every age as a result of the trust and good will by which all fairy tale heroes are tested.

As the Mother Goose

wandered through history, world destiny unfolded, and the understanding of what the stars were speaking waned, giving way to the reason and logic of the hard sciences, including among them the science of astronomy. Charles Perrault's brother Claude, a famed architect who designed and built the façade along the east-facing wing of the Palais Louvre, also designed the Paris Observatory, today one of the largest national research centers for astronomy and the oldest existing operating observatory of the stars in the western hemisphere.

From our place in history it seems ironic that Louis XIV, the Sun King, commissioned the Observatory in the same year that he declared all the streets of Paris to be hung with lanterns. This is how Paris achieved its reputation as the "city of light," a beautiful idea that nonetheless revealed how far the stars had fallen: from the starry pillars of the Ancient Egyptians to the spoken tales of Bertrada; from the written word of Charles Perrault to a silencing by artificial light and the age of reason. Lighting up the night meant the stars would be lost, and with them, their stories. No longer would it be understood that letters were the sacred gift of the stars, discovered by the Muses and borne toward humanity on the wings of the celestial swan. It is as though this knowing, once it was written down, went into hiding on the page, which meant it could be dismissed as a wild imagination or "just a fairy tale."

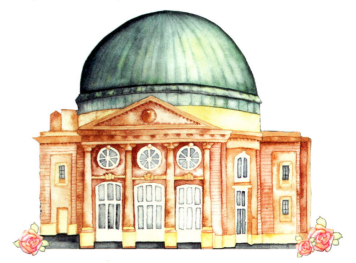

At this point in their becoming, the tales of Mother Goose were still fairy tales, not yet nursery rhymes, for the Swan Initiate had to swim the English Channel before she would become associated with the witty songstress of the nursery.

She arrived on the shores of England in 1729, in the form of Robert Samber's direct translation of Charles Perrault's Mother Goose Fairy Tales, and it wasn't until Thomas Carnan published his *Mother Goose's Melody or Sonnets for the Cradle* nearly 50 years later, in the 1780s, that she appeared solely as the mistress of the nursery rhyme.

Carnan was the stepson of the famous children's book publisher John Newbery, and like those before him, he didn't compose the rhymes, he gathered them and wrote them down.

The children's ditties Carnan attributed to his Mother Goose were those that were sung by children throughout the land, to which he added the lyrics of Shakespeare from nearly 200 years earlier, and by which means he established the Mother Goose that we know today. Once the tales and rhymes were written down, their potent connection to the mystery wisdom of the stars waned and became even more hidden.

In the meantime, in America, a legend developed regarding another Mother Goose, Elizabeth Foster Goose (1665-1758) of Boston. Elizabeth was the wife of Isaac Goose, and between them they had 16 children. When her husband died, Elizabeth went to live with her eldest daughter, who had married Thomas Fleet, a publisher in Pudding Lane. The legend is that Elizabeth used to sing songs and ditties to her grandchildren and eventually, Thomas wrote them down as the rhymes of Mother Goose. Alas, no such text exists and this legend is refuted by Mother Goose scholars.

The confusion rests in thinking of Mother Goose as an historical individual, rather than as a title for one who has achieved the Swan Initiation. Swan Initiates surrendered name and identity in order to more freely bear the moral wisdom that streams though time as the sacred resonance of all things that would be named, be they stars or princesses clad in glass slippers or old kings with blue beards, or even girls that lose sheep and cats that play fiddles.

John Newbery

There are many ways to imagine the passage of Mother Goose fairy tales and nursery rhymes across the great Atlantic after she first appeared on the page in 17th century France. Take, for instance, Benjamin Franklin, who exulted in and readily adopted the ways of his European forebears and hosts. He was the American Minister to France from 1777 to 1790, nearly a century after Perrault's Mother Goose tales were published there, and had been to London even earlier, in 1724, to train as a printer. By the time Franklin returned to London in 1757, John Newbery was already established as a publisher and bookseller, renowned for his children's books. Just as Franklin traveled back and forth across the great waters dividing the continents, so too traveled the French tales and English rhymes of Mother Goose, seamlessly weaving cultures together through story and rhyme in spite of revolution and war.

Benjamin Franklin

Though we would know differently here in the 21st century, the Sun, Moon, planets and all the stars still seem to be moving in beautiful, rhythmic array around the Earth, like elegantly dressed attendees to our theater in the round, where we unfold our human drama for all the cosmos to see. The world is our stage, onto which we have fallen from these starry worlds, and we are as players for this celestial audience, the stars themselves, who gather each night to watch this great human drama in its various acts. Like all audiences, the stars wait on the delightful experience of finding themselves woven into our human drama, while hiding out in our experience, playing bo peep at every turn,

surrendering themselves in order to assist us in our becoming, so that, out of our own striving, we will remember the joy and delight with which we descended from their world into our own.

Once upon a time, the stars spoke to human beings. They spoke the true names of everything that is. Through time and the destiny of our own becoming, they grew silent, until now. Now they wait for us to remember, and to sing their names in return, through story and rhyme and every way imaginable, and through our song, to share with them what it is to be a human being. This is the only way they will ever know this world—through the joyful hearts of human beings that have opened to the abundant good will pouring unto us from the heaven's brink.

The Star Tales of Mother Goose

Part II

Star Verses by Mary Stewart Adams
With History, Guides & Maps

As the ability to understand the speaking of the stars faded through the ages, nursery rhymes and fairy tales began to spring up, bouncing along with whimsy and rhyme and once upon a time towards happily ever after.

To those bereft of star knowledge yet rich with imagination, these rhymes and tales revealed a secret language that warmed their hearts, the same way beautiful star shine lights up the otherwise dark unknown that lurks in the night.

Joining these rhymes to the stars that playfully hide within them has been the work of

the Star Lore Historian

and her tales go something like this....

There was a song of sixpence
Star rhyme

With our days four and twenty
As the sun takes the sky,
There are those who will use it
To simply make pie!
The king, in his house, counts his money so bold,
The queen, in her parlor
Spreads her muffins with gold,
And the maiden, she's busy,
The sheets for to fold.
But what's hidden there in this scene so sweet,
Is the thing that can happen with a
    Moon at your feet!
Then the maid rises up
Wearing the crown of the sky
Placed among kings as the dragon goes by.

HISTORY AND STARS
SING A SONG OF SIXPENCE

The delightful sixpence ditty was originally sung in celebration of the "entremet"—from the Old French meaning "between servings"—an entertainment dish common among the nobility in Europe in the later parts of the Middle Ages. A sort of mood and palette cleanser between courses, the entremet developed over time from simple porridges that were colored and flavored with exotic spices to elaborate models of castles with wine fountains and musicians, and even live birds placed in baked pie shells, so that when the pie was opened, the birds fluttered out singing into the dining hall.

When we look for the stars in this ditty, we find the King in his counting house is Cepheus, the constellation of the king, standing there in the night sky with his foot on the Milky Way—the Milky Way is his counting house, and the treasure trove of stars is his money. The Queen is our Cassiopeia, whose golden honey she gathers from the beehive cluster (known as M44 to astronomers) at the heart of the constellation Cancer. The maid who's hanging out the clothes is the lovely Virgo, who appears reclining on the ecliptic, the path that the Sun, Moon and planets seem to follow around the Earth. All the constellations of the zodiac are located here. This ecliptic path is the maid's clothesline.

And the blackbird that tweaks off her nose? That's Corvus, the crow, rising up from just beneath Virgo, where he is stationed on the back of the water serpent Hydra.

When Virgo is imagined in an upright position, as the Ancient Egyptians saw her several thousand years ago, rather than reclining, as she was later imagined by the Ancient Greeks, then we find the constellation of the starry crown, Corona Borealis, appearing at her head. The mystery of the maiden rising up on the Moon to achieve the starry crown causes the serpent Hydra to stir from his slumber beneath her, and recalls the mighty imagination of a woman, clothed with the Sun, the Moon beneath her feet, a crown of stars upon her head.

MOON

While there is typically one full moon each month, the vernal full moon is exceptional because it is the first full moon of the year to appear below the celestial equator, which is the Earth's equator projected into space so as to distinguish between northern and southern celestial hemispheres. This full moon happens in the region of Virgo stars, where the celestial equator crosses the path of the ecliptic (the clothesline). Because of this the vernal full moon could also be called the "Moon beneath the feet of the maiden, Virgo," and it is used by many cultures to establish the date for the sacred festivals of renewal in the spring.

Sing a Song of Sixpence
A Guide to the Stars

Cepheus and Cassiopeia are members of the royal family which continuously circle around the North Star. As the Queen, Cassiopeia enjoys the reputation of being one of the most recognized constellations in the sky, especially because her stars seems to make the pattern of a large "W." Cepheus is not so easy to find because his stars are less bright, but there he is beside the Milky Way, nearly standing on the North Pole.

To find your way to the stars in our rhyme, begin with the Big Dipper asterism in the constellation of the Great Bear. Facing north on April nights, the Dipper will appear with its cup open toward the northern horizon, its handle arcing toward the east and the bright star Arcturus. Follow the two stars on the outside lip of the Dipper's cup to the North Star, Polaris. A straight line from this star points to the star Errai, the "shepherd" star that marks the left foot of Cepheus. His shape is like a little house, and the Milky Way appears to sweep over his left shoulder.

To find Cassiopeia, follow the two stars that form the handle-side of the Big Dipper's cup to the North Star, and continue straight to Caph, the star that marks the upper corner of Cassiopeia's throne.

Cassiopeia is eating honey from the beehive cluster at the heart of Cancer in our rhyme. Like Cepheus, Cancer is not made up of bright stars, but to get there, imagine the Big Dipper sprang a leak in the middle of its cup. The water would drip drip drip on to the back of Leo, the lion. Leo's brightest star is Regulus, which is high up overhead on April nights. Regulus forms an isosceles triangle with the bright star Pollux just north of west, and Procyon, just south of west. The constellation Cancer appears at the center of this triangle.

Finding the maid and the blackbird is quite a bit easier. Again, beginning with the Big Dipper, follow the arc of its handle to the bright star Arcturus. Continuing the arc, speed on to Spica, the bright star in the constellation of the maiden, Virgo. Following the arc further will lead you to the constellation Corvus, the black bird that nips off her nose!

Star Seeker's Key

CEPHEUS
King

MILKY WAY
Counting House

CASSIOPEIA
Queen

BEEHIVE CLUSTER IN THE REGION OF CANCER
Honey, an open star cluster also known as Praësepe and Messier #44

VIRGO
Maid

ECLIPTIC PATH OF THE PLANETS
Clothesline

CORVUS
Blackbird

HYDRA
Serpent

CORONA BOREALIS
Starry Crown

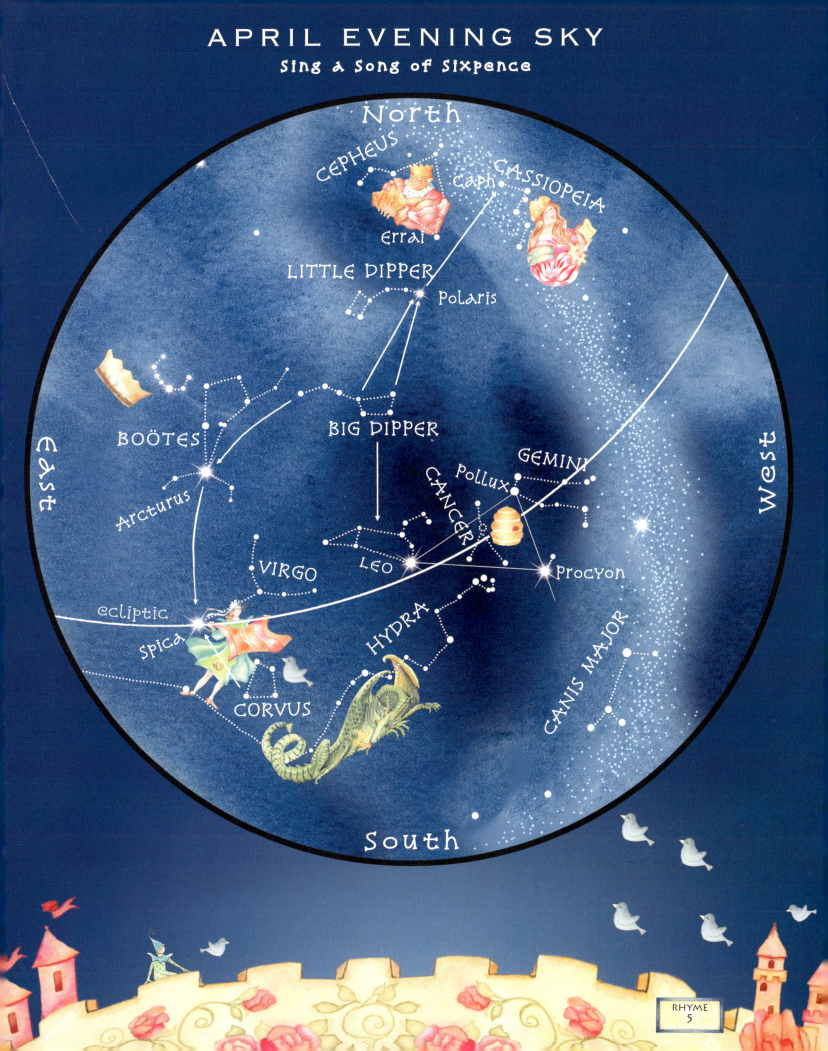

THE LION AND THE UNICORN
STAR RHYME

There once was a lion and unicorn
in station beneath the crown,
You can see them still in the starry sky
When the vernal sun goes down.
Some say they would fight for that royal piece
As they traveled across the sky,
And the men and the countries lying beneath
Would rise up with a rallying cry!
For the lion is England's
emblem bold
and the unicorn
herald of Scots,
& ne'er were fiercer stories told
of bold and curious plots.

History and Stars
The Lion and the Unicorn

In the 1600s, as the Italian astronomer Galileo was first using his telescope to discover new worlds in the heavens above, there were brave souls that dared to sail off the edge of the known world. This was like venturing into the realm of dragons, but lo!, what they found instead were new features of the sky.

These sailors and explorers saw groups of stars that never appeared in the heavens of their homelands, and so the race was on to create new constellations. Eventually this race included not only the new stars over the new lands they were discovering, but those familiar stars that lacked definition by the ancient sages who had crafted the books and maps that dominated the star knowledge of the centuries.

The trick to getting a new constellation to stick was to be well connected, so that the map makers would include your patterns on their charts and in their atlases. Enter the son-in-law of famous astronomer Johannes Kepler, Jakob Bartsch, who, in 1613, depicted six such new constellations based on the work of Petrus Plancius. Despite their popularity in the 17th century, only two of these constellations are still recognized today: Camelopardalis, the giraffe; and Monoceros, the unicorn. There were no originating myths connected with these new constellations the way there were with the original 48 starry regions of the ancient world ~ they endured through popularity and practicality.

Around this same time, there were new developments in Britain when, in 1603, the Union of the Crowns was enacted, by which King James VI of Scotland inherited the English throne from his double-first-cousin-twice-removed, Queen Elizabeth I. In effect, this meant that the two independent kingdoms of England and Scotland shared a monarch, although to be clear, at this time there were two separate crowns resting on the same royal head.

There were several attempts to unite the two kingdoms by parliamentary Acts of Union in the 1600s, but this was not achieved until a great deal of turmoil gave way to the next century. Only after 1707 can we finally speak of a United Kingdom, and the traditional verse of the Lion and the Unicorn is published, by William King.

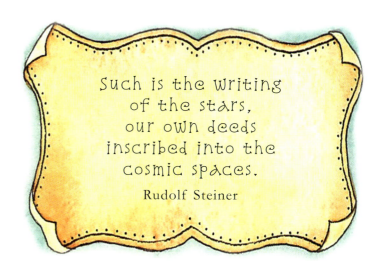

Such is the writing of the stars, our own deeds inscribed into the cosmic spaces.
Rudolf Steiner

The Lion and the Unicorn
A GUIDE TO THE STARS

Star Seeker's Key

LEO
Lion/Herald of England

MONOCEROS
Unicorn/Herald of Scotand

CORONA BOREALIS
Crown

The royal emblems of Great Britain rise up into the April sky where the King and Queen that we met in Sixpence are continuously watching over, joined by the constellation of Corona Borealis, the starry crown.

To find your way to the constellations in our rhyme, face north and identify the Big Dipper asterism. Follow the arc of the Big Dipper's handle to the east, and you will see that it arcs toward the bright star Arcturus. From Arcturus, take a short hop north and a skip east to the star Gemma, which is the jewel in the center of the starry crown. The starry crown is sometimes referred to as the golden diadem, because it appears to make the shape of a soft "u" northward from the star Gemma, like a tiara. The creatures in our rhyme are battling one another for this royal piece.

The Lion is nearly straight overhead in April, and can be found beneath the cup of the Big Dipper. The brightest star in Leo has the name Regulus, and a line imagined from Regulus toward the brightest star just south of west leads to Procyon, and puts you in the vicinity of Monoceros, the unicorn. From Procyon, imagine a straight line south to Sirius, the brightest nighttime star in our sky. Such a line would pass right through the hindquarters of the unicorn. Don't get frustrated if you can't see it—the stars here are rather like the unicorn itself, difficult to find!

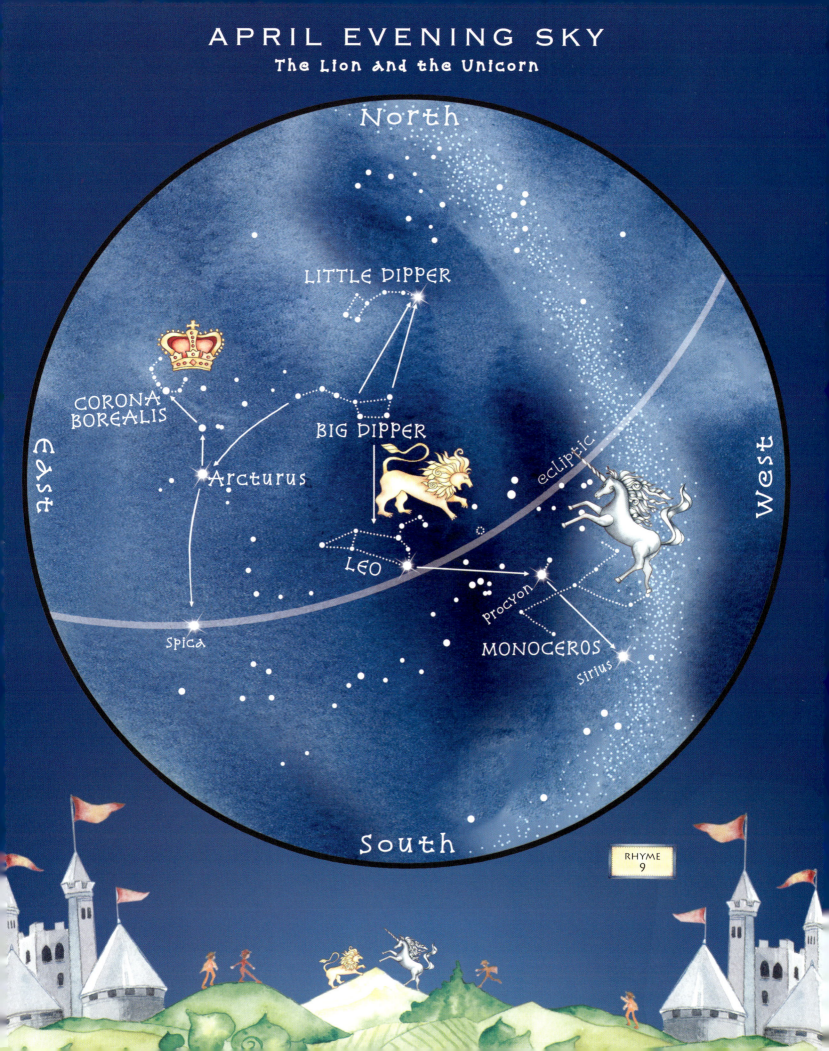

HEY DIDDLE DIDDLE
STAR RHYME

Beyond the swan and with the swan,
beside the fair old maid,
The lion chases the little dog
Over the earth in May
The maestro tunes his fiddle and bow,
And the Milky Way disappears,
I would scoop it up with my spoon, you know,
But only song would the waking king hear!
For when Luna is nigh on the Pleiades,
Those maidens a-fair on the wing,
The starry Bull lifts his fiery head
And in ditty must I sing:

So hey diddle, oh diddle,
See yon cat, hear yon fiddle!
There's a cow jumping over the Moon.
The little dog laughs to see such a sport
And the Milky Way dish runs away
With the spoon!

History and Stars
Hey Diddle Diddle

Every year in May when the Moon is new among the stars of Taurus, the orbiting Earth dips forward through the starry light to a position that gives us a sky view that is perpendicular to the plane of our galaxy, with the result that the stars of the Milky Way seem to disappear beyond the edge of the horizon—it's as though the Milky Way is flat like a dish at such times, and it disappears, or "runs away" from view. The Big Dipper is directly overhead, appearing every bit like a celestial spoon, a maestro of the stars, striking up a starry tune from the fiddle, our constellation Lyra in the east, and calling forth the big cat, Leo, to chase the little dog, Canis Minor, out of the sky to the west. This makes way for Cygnus the swan, that old mother goose, who flaps her mighty wings from her as-yet-hidden place along the Milky Way of stars.

What's tucked into the seeming nonsense of this 16th century rhyme of Thomas Preston and Alexander Montgomerie?

The ancients of nearly every culture believed that the human soul does not originate with the Earth but descends from the stars—each one from a particular star. In this picture the zodiac of stars that appears to embrace the Earth is imagined as the outer vestige of mighty celestial beings that had the sacred role of forming the human physical body in preparation for its receiving this soul. To this incarnating soul they imparted unique gifts, the way fairy godmothers do when they are called to participate in fairy tale christenings for fairy tale princesses with fairy tale kings and queens in fairy tales throughout the world.

It is out of this world view that ancient cultures developed the understanding that each region of the zodiac bears relationship to specific members of the human physical form. The region of Taurus stars is related to the human speech organ, the larynx. Ancient Egyptian art depicts how the larynx was as though formed by the guidance of wise beings, which imparted to the human being the divine gift of the word, which rises up with feeling from the heart and joins with the thinking of the head, to be uttered forth with creative power in the world. Exercising this wisdom is described as the first deed of the first beings in various cultures, including in the Ancient Greek, where the Titan Mnemosyne, goddess of memory and mother of the Muses, gave a designation to every object; and in the Genesis story of Adam, who is given power to name all things that are. Designating every object is of the utmost importance, since without names, very little could be understood in the world.

The Moon makes its way through Taurus stars every month, but only once each year does the Moon achieve its New Phase in this region of the starry bull, signaling that the time is right, the celestial harmony is struck, and with our words we can once again give voice to what lies on our hearts, with a hey diddle diddle!

Hey Diddle Diddle
A GUIDE TO THE STARS

Star Seeker's Key

LEO
Cat

LYRA
Fiddle

TAURUS
Cow

MOON
New among the stars of Taurus in May

CANIS MINOR
Little Dog

MILKY WAY
Dish

BIG DIPPER
Spoon

The Sun rises and sets with the stars of Taurus in the month of May, so though we can imagine the cow jumping over the New Moon as in our rhyme, we won't see it in the sky. At the time of night in the northern hemisphere shown on our map, Taurus has already set with the Sun in the west.

To find the rest of the characters, locate the Big Dipper overhead, its cup open to the north, and its handle arcing to the east, toward the bright star Arcturus. The Dipper is our spoon.

Look northeast from Arcturus to the blue-white star Vega, the brightest star in the constellation Lyra, which is the fiddle in our rhyme.

Returning to the Dipper, remember that if it sprang a leak, it would drip on the back of Leo, our celestial, musical cat, who can be seen chasing the little dog, Canis Minor, over the western-most edge of the sky.

The dish in Hey Diddle Diddle can be imagined as the Milky Way, which is flat around the horizon in May, and its running away in the rhyme is not just errant behavior, it actually means that when the spoon is directly overhead, then we have a view perpendicular to our galaxy. This means we don't see the Milky Way so well, because it's flat around the horizon and disappears from view.

LITTLE BO PEEP
STAR RHYME

Have you ever been told when
    you're trying to sleep
That it's best to start counting
    some fat little sheep?
You can find them up there
    as they're circling by,
Where Bo Peep is chasing them
    all through the sky.

They pretend that they're
    bears and they don't
    stay in place,
Circling around without
    leaving a trace!
But look for their tails,
    you'll find them, I know,
Then Bo Peep she can herd
    them, all in a neat row.
For they always come home,
    no matter how far,
'cause always they're circling
    their favorite north star.

History and Stars
LITTLE BO PEEP

The first historical use of the term "bo peep" seems to have been in the 14th century, in reference to a type of punishment known as being stood in a pillory, a wooden framework with holes for the head and arms, usually erected in a public place. The record of the day describes how a poor ale wife was short-changing her customers and was forced to "play bo pepe, thorowe a pillery."

To "play bo peep" still meant the same thing 200 years later, only now references to sheep had entered into the description, as though to stand with your head poking through the stocks was to be like a sheep sticking its head through a fence row to get the greener grass on the other side. In the first act of Shakespeare's "King Lear," to play "bo peep" meant to play a game of peek-a-boo. Finally in the 19th century, the first printed version of the traditional verse appeared.

Between the first recorded reference of Bo Peep in the 14th century and the first publication of the full verse in the 19th century, human concepts regarding the world completely changed, and the Copernican idea that the Earth was in motion around the Sun began to take hold. This introduced new ideas and new terms into the language, including, in the 1680s, the word "circumpolar" which is a word used to describe bodies that are continually visible above the horizon—they literally circle (circum-) the Pole Star (-polar).

Every night in the northern hemisphere, there are five of these circumpolar constellations overhead: a king, a queen, two bears, and a dragon, moving round and round through the sky, never disappearing from the nightscape as they circle the Pole Star, Polaris, at the tip of the Little Dipper's handle.

Nearby this quintet, but technically not circumpolar, is the constellation Boötes. Boötes was first named by Homer in his Odyssey as a celestial reference point for navigation, and was known in many traditions as the "bear herder" because he seems to herd both the bears, Ursa Major and Minor, around the Pole Star.

But who ever heard of a bear herder? And come to think of it, who ever heard of bears with such long tails?

Scratching the surface of the star names in the circumpolar region of the sky reveals that there are many starry references here to sheep, like Alioth in the Big Dipper's handle, which means "the fat tail end of the eastern sheep," and Alderamin in Cepheus, which means "flock"; Errai, also in the region of Cepheus, means "shepherd"; and "Kappa Cephei" means "lost sheep." So instead of being a bear herder, Boötes could rightfully be referred to as a sheep herder, and the Bears, Ursas Major and Minor, are his sheep. Then, rather than considering the constellation a "male" named Boötes, we find instead a little girl named Bo Peep, who has lost her sheep, because they keep circling away from her through the sky.

CIRCUMPOLARITY

Cleverly tucked into this little nonsense rhyme is the concept of circumpolarity, and the lovely reassurance that comes from the harmony of the circling stars, that Little Bo Peep need not worry about her sheep, she can even leave them alone because they'll always come home, wagging their tails behind them.

Little Bo Peep
A GUIDE TO THE STARS

Star Seeker's Key

BOÖTES
Bo Peep

URSA MAJOR (Big Dipper), URSA MINOR (Little Dipper)
Sheep

ALIOTH (first star in handle of Big Dipper)
Fat Tail end of the eastern sheep

ALDERAMIN
Flock

ERRAI
Shepherd

KAPPA CEPHEI
Lost Sheep

The constellation characters of Bo Peep circle overhead nearly every night in the Northern Hemisphere, expect for Boötes, who seems to set for a short time in the colder months. To find your way to Bo Peep and her sheep, locate the Big Dipper, just east of the zenith, its cup open toward the north. The Big Dipper can be imagined as one of Bo Peep's sheep, and from the Dipper, we can find another one of the sheep, and the shepherdess herself.

Follow the arc of the Big Dipper's handle to the star Arcturus. This is the brightest star in the constellation Boötes, which we imagine is the Bo Peep of our rhyme.

Also from the Big Dipper, imagine a straight line headed north through the pointer stars Merak and Dubhe, which mark the outside lip of the Dipper's cup. These two point directly to Polaris, our north star, at the end of the handle or tail of the Little Dipper. Don't be fooled, *the North Star is important, but it's not very bright.* Best to look before it gets too dark and Polaris gets harder to find.

Since Cepheus contains some of the "sheep" stars, best to find him, too, with a hop skip from the Little Dipper aiming further north. Cepheus looks like an upside down house, midway along a line drawn from Polaris to Cassiopeia. The constellation Boötes-Bo Peep hosts a gentle meteor each year at the end of June.

LITTLE BOY BLUE
STAR RHYME

There's a hero up there upside down in the sky,

As the Milky Way rises and the cow goes by,

We call him Boy Blue down here on the ground,

Where Bo Peep cries out for her sheep to be found!

And though he seems lazy and awfully shy

He's bearing a mystery across the sky:

Star-born and royal he reminds us are we,

And when we awake,

then heroes we'll be!

History and Stars
Little Boy Blue

When the cow wanders away in the meadow of stars beyond the western edge of the world each spring, then it's time to look east, where the mysteries of the season are hidden. There we find the faint constellation of the Kneeler, or Hercules to the ancients, appearing upside down on bent knee, rising up through the night, beneath the Milky Way. The Dippers have wheeled counter-clockwise along on the mighty timepiece of the night, and our Little Bo Peep is aloft with her crook, casting wishes across the sky like falling stars.

The faintness of the stars and the upside down position of the Kneeler makes the clever stargazer wonder why the Ancient Greeks and Romans would associate this constellation with their mighty hero. After all, Hercules, Herakles to the Greeks, was a son of Zeus and he handily accomplished the 12 labors assigned to him by his jealous older brother. Clearly there's something more than meets the eye in this constellation, just as there is in our rhyme of the little Boy Blue who is fast asleep. The rhyme was first printed in *Tommy Thumb's Little Song Book* (c. 1744), but it may be much older, and may even be alluded to in Shakespeare's "King Lear" over a century earlier, in 1606.

The ancient myth of Hercules, the configuration of the constellation, and the sleeping boy blue all reveal the ages-old belief in the human being's higher nature, which has its origin among the stars and is often described as slumbering within. The task of awakening this higher, star-born self is like wrestling with the giant, the human being's lower, Earth-bound nature. Hercules appears upside down because he is rooted in the stars, not the Earth, and he represents the quest to take up the path to self knowledge. Until we take up the path of our own labors that lead to this self knowledge, we sleep, and while we sleep, the cows take the meadow, and the sheep take the corn!

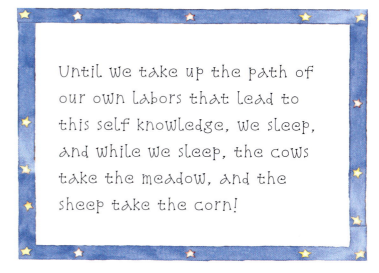

> Until we take up the path of our own labors that lead to this self knowledge, we sleep, and while we sleep, the cows take the meadow, and the sheep take the corn!

Here's how this ditty is connected to the ancient myth: On his way from retrieving the golden apples from the garden of the Hesperides, Hercules passed through Libya, where he encountered the giant Anteaus. Antaeus was a son of Poseidon, god of Oceans, and Gaia, the Earth Mother. Anteaus' secret power lay in his connection to the Earth, and he forced all passersby to wrestle on the ground, knowing he would be undefeated. To master him, Hercules simply lifted him off the ground and held him aloft until he perished. Here we find another clue that Hercules is akin to the human being's higher nature, which, with diligence, can overcome the lower, Earth-bound self, represented by Anteaus.

Little Boy Blue
A GUIDE TO THE STARS

Star Seeker's Key

HERCULES (also know as The Kneeler)
Boy Blue, his upside down nature revealing he is rooted in the stars

MILKY WAY
Haystack

TAURUS
Cow, which sets by the time Hercules rises

DIPPERS
Sheep (see Bo Peep)

THE STAR SPICA
In the constellation **VIRGO**, corn associated with the Goddess of the Harvest

In *The Star Tales of Mother Goose* we imagine the sleeping Little Boy Blue as the constellation Hercules, upside down just west of the Milky Way where it starts to rise in the east. The best way to find him is to locate the Big Dipper overhead, and follow the arc of its handle to the bright star Arcturus, in the constellation Boötes. A line drawn from Arcturus northeast to the beautiful star Vega will pass right through the torso of Hercules, sometimes referred to as the "keystone." Remember he's upside down, and his hips are wider than his shoulders.

The sheep we have already imagined as the Dippers, from Little Bo Peep's rhyme, and the corn is represented by the star Spica in the constellation Virgo. To find Spica, begin at the Big Dipper, follow the arc of its handle to Arcturus, and from there, speed on to Spica, alone in the south on May evenings.

The cow we imagine as Taurus, which has wandered away with the Sun, over the western edge of the world.

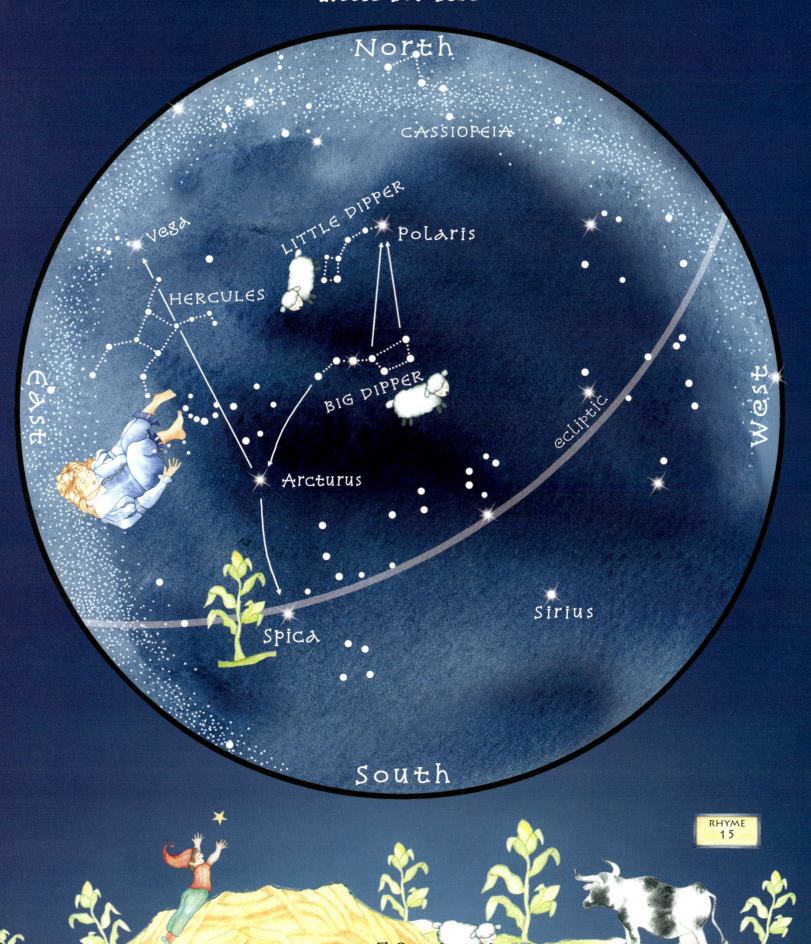

Old Humpty he fell off the wall, you see,

But he's not just an egg to you and to me!

He's really the sun rolling right through the sky

'Til he sits on the wall

that is awfully high.

He pauses a bit

when he gets to that spot

But stay there forever he must certainly not!

His horses rise up and so do his men,

To help him roll off to the south, again.

So as you watch for Humpty up there in the sky,

He's sometimes quite low and other times high,

And always he's shining as he goes rolling by.

History and Stars
HUMPTY DUMPTY

Nursery rhymes are the best hiding places for clever riddles, and Humpty Dumpty is no exception. As one of the best-known nursery rhymes in the English-speaking world, Humpty Dumpty is often portrayed as an egg, as though he were a short, clumsy, fragile person, and those are the only clues. But a peek into starry worlds suggests that there's a whole lot more going on here than meets the eye, or puzzles the mind and tickles the funny bone!

As mentioned above, the Sun appears to travel along the ecliptic, rising and setting as it goes, sometimes north, sometimes south. Before it changes its course north or south, the Sun appears to pause, the same way a human being pauses between inhalation and exhalation in breathing. These pauses are called the solstices, which means the Sun (Sol-) stands still (-stice), and they happen when the Sun is highest above or furthest below the celestial equator.

So where's the riddle in all of this, and what does it have to do with Humpty Dumpty? The earliest known version of this riddling rhyme was published in 1791, when the idea of the Earth in motion about the Sun had already taken hold. But if instead we imagine Humpty Dumpty is the Sun in motion about the Earth, then we can also imagine that when he makes his merry way through the stars to the point highest above the celestial equator where he pauses, it's as though he's sitting on the wall. From that solstice wall Humpty has no choice but to fall forward toward the celestial equator and to autumn equinox. And when the Humpty Dumpty Sun begins his fall toward equinox, then the constellations of the "king's horses" and the "king's men" begin to rise up in the night. They can't put the Humpty Sun together again upon the solstice wall because they can't turn back the course of time!

Humpty must follow his course forward through the year, or else release chaos in all the worlds—and that would be no fun for such a merry shining fellow, who prefers to leave a trail of ditties in his wake as he carries the light from the top of the sky.

61

Humpty Dumpty
A GUIDE TO THE STARS

Star Seeker's Key

THE SUN
Humpty Dumpty

SUMMER SOLSTICE
The Wall, the moment when the sun stands still highest above the Celestial Equator

PEGASUS, EQUULEUS
King's Horses

BOÖTES, HERCULES, PERSEUS
King's Men

In order to identify the region of stars where they are doing their research, astronomers draw imaginary lines in space. These lines are based on the Earth as the central point of reference, and make use of two things that we know but that we can't actually see: the Earth's equator, and the path of the planets. Astronomers call these lines in space the celestial equator and the ecliptic, respectively.

We don't see these lines, but we can draw them on a map. But first, let's imagine the Earth at the center of a mighty celestial sphere of stars. To distinguish the top from the bottom of this sphere, or the north from the south, we project the Earth's equator onto it. Now we have the celestial equator.

Next, we can chart the apparent path of the planets along this sphere. It seems to us on Earth that everything is moving around us in space, including the Sun and the Moon, and if we watch closely through the years, we find that they, together with all the planets, keep to a particular path among the stars as they move about us, never straying from this path, but following their rhythmic course. We call this path the ecliptic.

The path of the planets, the ecliptic, is not coincident with the celestial equator, but because they both seem to go around us on the Earth, we find them crossing at two points. At these two points, it is as though everything is harmoniously aligned, and when the Sun appears at either one of these points, we experience equal day and night on Earth. We call these points the moments of equinox, and they occur at the onset of spring and fall each year.

There are also two points where the paths are furthest apart from one another, where the ecliptic is highest above or furthest below the celestial equator. When the Sun arrives at either of these points, we experience the longest days and the shortest days of the year. We call these moments the solstices, and they mark the onset of summer and winter.

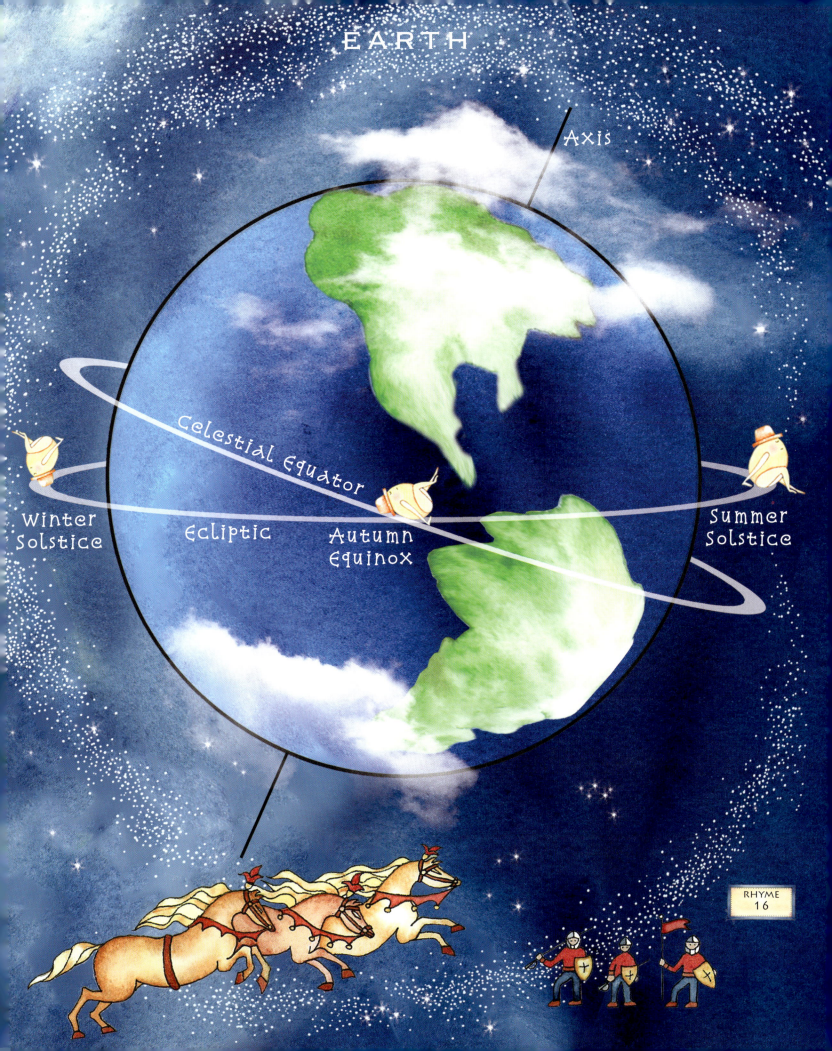

As the mighty heart at the center of our planetary system, the Sun outshines everything in the sky. Because of this, we don't see the stars beyond the Sun at its solstice and equinox moments.

Here the Humpty Dumpty Sun makes sport along the ecliptic, to help identify where the Sun is at equinox, when it crosses the celestial equator; and when it stands still highest above or furthest below this same imaginary line at its solstices.

Throughout history and around the world, these moments have always marked the most sacred times of the year.

MOTHER GOOSE
STAR RHYME

There's an Old Mother Goose

    taking wing through the sky,

Carrying wishes and dreams

    to the stars on high,

She greets every star,

    and they dance and they sing,

Then back down to Earth

    their riches she brings.

History and Stars
Mother Goose

Once upon a time there were two brothers who worked in the service of a mighty king. So mighty was the King, he was known throughout the land as the Sun King, and though he had elaborate palaces with ornate furnishings, he wanted more.

He summoned the older brother. "Build me a palace that faces east, so that the Sun and I may greet one another each day with the dawn." And so the palace was built.

But still the Sun King wanted more.

Once again he summoned the older brother. "I would have a house of stars so that I may reach deeply into the night, in anticipation of the Sun before he rises." And the house of stars was built.

Around this time, a cold swept through the kingdom and all the surrounding lands. The Sun had grown quiet, its warming rays no longer drawing life up out of the Earth as they always had. This angered the Sun King, so he summoned the younger brother, a man of letters. "Write a proclamation to the Sun, commanding that he restore his warmth to my kingdom." The younger brother begged pardon of the King, suggesting that perhaps such a proclamation was not the way to address the Sun. But the King insisted, "For," said he, "am I not also the Sun King?"

Mindful of his service to the King, but true to the greater role of the Sun, the younger brother wrote the proclamation. At the same time, he also wrote something more, secret missives in which he hid his knowledge of the stars. These missives spoke a secret language that restored warmth to the people throughout the kingdom, in spite of the ongoing cold caused by the quiet Sun and the loud commands of the King.

Eventually, the Sun resumed its natural activity and warmth, but the Sun King grew old and died. And though the younger brother's missives were well loved, eventually their secrets were no longer understood, and they were dismissed as nonsense tales and make believe.

The Sun King is known to history as Louis XIV, who reigned in France from 1643 to 1715, during which time an unusually prolonged minimum occurred in sunspot activity, from 1645 to 1715. This same period also coincided with lower-than-average temperatures throughout Europe.

The two brothers are Claude and Charles Perrault. Claude was an architect, while his younger brother Charles was a man of letters. In 1695, just a few years after a star exploded near the beak of the Swan constellation, Cygnus, Charles Perrault published his first book: *Tales from the Past with Morals, the Tales of Mother Goose*.

Over 300 years later, two sisters took up the story of these two brothers, inspired by a message that swept through the ages on the wings of a dream. The great mystery pronounced that Mother Goose is Cygnus. This message led to the book that you now hold in your hands.

Mother Goose
A GUIDE TO THE STARS

Star Seeker's Key

CYGNUS
Mother Goose

SUMMER TRIANGLE
Deneb, the tail star of Cygnus is part of the Summer Triangle, which also includes Vega, and Altair

MILKY WAY
On August nights Cygnus flies overhead from the North to the South along the Milky Way river of stars

To find Cygnus you can begin by looking for the mighty Summer Triangle of stars in the sky, which are some of the first to appear on Summer evenings, rising up in the east as summer begins. The Summer Triangle makes its way to the top of the sky in August, when the thickest region of the Milky Way also becomes visible in northern hemisphere skies.

You can also find Cygnus by first identifying the star Arcturus, a campfire orange star that appears high in the west on August nights. Looking due east from Arcturus, across the top of the sky, brings you to the blue-white star Vega in the constellation Lyra. From Vega looking south and slightly east, you will begin to see Altair; while looking north and east of Vega, you will find Deneb. Notice that these three stars will appear during the twilight time, and can be used as guides for where the Milky Way will appear, once the sky is dark enough.

From the tail star Deneb, Cygnus appears to fly south, as though into the center of the Summer Triangle. The beak of Cygnus is marked by the beautiful double-star system Albireo, which is a telescopic treat. It was near this star that a nova appeared in the late 1600s, during the same era in which Charles Perrault published his *Tales of Mother Goose*.

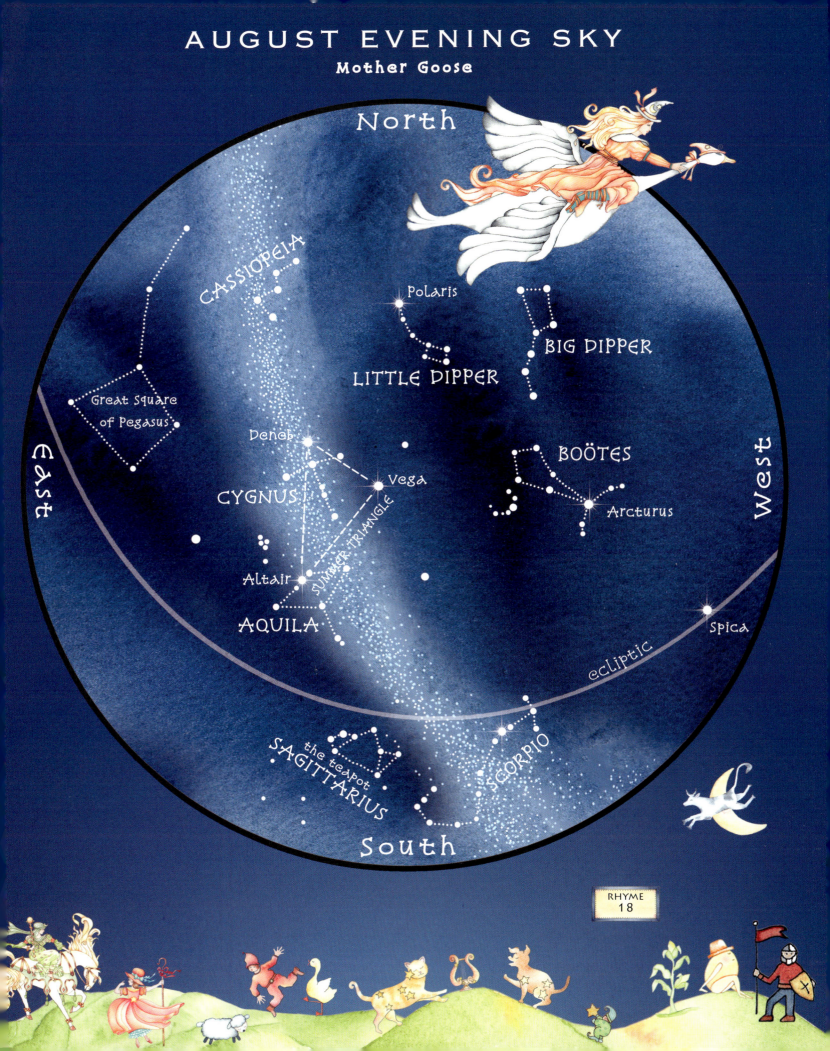

OLD KING COLE
STAR RHYME

Twice every year

when day equals night,

the king lifts his heels

in a dance of delight

and summons his players,

from left and from right.

History and Stars
OLD KING COLE

Although the historical origins of King Cole are speculative, his merry place among the stars is not! For there he sits, high on his throne in the Milky Way as the constellation Cepheus, the king, one foot firm on the Milky Way of stars, the other steadying the "solstitial colure," that great circle of the heavens described as a line drawn from solstice point to solstice point, through the North Star.

Cepheus is not a constellation of bright and easy stars, and he usually plays second fiddle to his consort and Queen Cassiopeia. Nonetheless, there are moments throughout the year when it's easy to imagine the Sun pausing a bit to greet the king, who then strikes up the band in a merry salute, calling for his pipe, the constellation Sagitta; his bowl, Corona Borealis; and his fiddler, Lyra; while in his hand he bears the garnet star, the most richly colored of all the stars in the sky. As king he is well aware that the more abundantly the harmony of the cosmos fills the soul, the more peace and harmony there will be on the earth, and such is his merry gift, from pole to starry pole.

The traditional ditty of Old King Cole seems to have first appeared in the 1700s, and while there are historical accounts of several Coles throughout history, it is just so that his merry origins are obscure, as it is with all the best things.

Old King Cole
A GUIDE TO THE STARS

Star Seeker's Key

CEPHEUS
King Cole

SAGITTA
Pipe

CORONA BOREALIS
Bowl

LYRA
Fiddler

King Cole provides one of the jolliest ways to get around the autumn sky, twinkling up there nearly at the zenith, and calling for music and dancing all around. To find your way to King Cole's dance, set out around 9 p.m. local time, and look north for the Big Dipper. Following the arc of its handle leads you to the bright star Arcturus, which is setting into the western horizon. One star above and one star west of Arcturus leads you to Gemma, in the constellation of Corona Borealis, the starry crown that serves as the bowl in King Cole's rhyme.

Back up to the Big Dipper, follow the pointer stars to Polaris, then continue on toward Cassiopeia, no wall flower at the king's dance, since her stars are much brighter than his. About halfway along a line drawn from Polaris to Cassiopeia is the tip of the king's constellation, which actually marks his left foot.

Sagitta, the King's pipe, is a tiny constellation (there are only two constellations of all 88 that are smaller), hiding out in the Altair corner of the Summer Triangle.

The fiddlers we imagine as the constellation Lyra, the lyre for the ancient Greeks but the fiddle in Bohemia. Lyra's brightest star Vega marks one corner of the Summer Triangle, still prominent in October skies, though summer has given way to fall.

OCTOBER EVENING SKY
Old King Cole

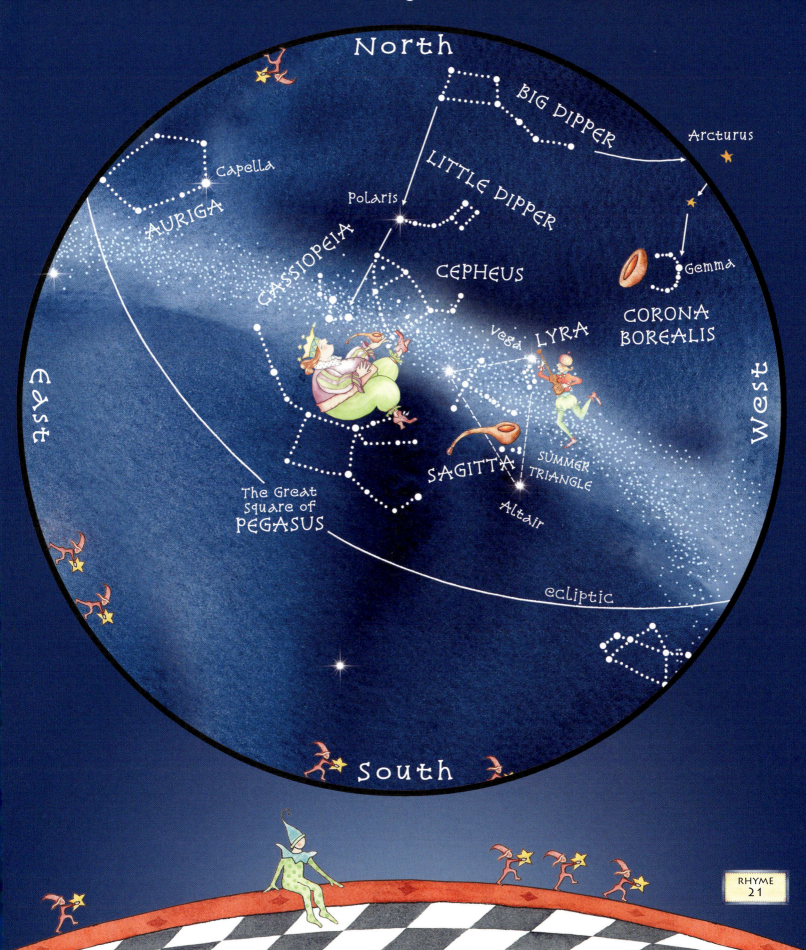

BANBURY CROSS
STAR RHYME

With tinkling and jostling and a heavenly rattle,
the fine lady sits high and proud in her saddle.
The horse trots a bit with his head held high,
bearing his lady across the sky,
With rings on her fingers and bells on her toes,
she brings joy with her music
                wherever she goes!

History and Stars
Banbury Cross

While our Fine Lady has obvious ties to place through her association with historic Banbury in Oxfordshire, England, she has deep roots in legends and stars as well—and if you meet a fine lady upon a white horse at a crossroads, be aware that you have arrived at the meeting place of worlds.

Banbury was established along the banks of the River Cherwell late in the 5th century at the junction of two ancient roads, at what are now known as the Salt Way, part of a medieval network of salt distribution routes, and Banbury Lane. It wasn't until 1784 that the Fine Lady's ride to the Cross here first appeared as a ditty, in Joseph Ritson's *The Nursery of Parnassus—A Choice Collection of Pretty Songs and Verses for the Amusement of all Little Good Children Who can Neither Read nor Run*. But long before the Nursery Parnassus, there were hints of the Fine Lady in verses and romances, such as the immensely popular "Floris and Blanchefleur" of the late 13th century, and tales of the Welsh Mabinogion of the same period.

The Mabinogion are the earliest prose stories of the literature of Britain, compiled in Middle Welsh from oral traditions. Here we find dramatic tales of Rhiannon, a strong-minded woman of other worlds, uniquely associated with horses, and with the Gaulish horse goddess Epona. Rhiannon and her son are often depicted as mare and foal, and she is shown sitting high on her horse in a calm, static pose. Upon her horse, Rhiannon led souls in the after-life ride, because she had access to the great starry worlds beyond.

In the romance of Floris and Blanchefleur of the same era, a fine horse and magic ring figure significantly in the settling of affairs into their happily ever after.

In the tale the king is in possession of a unique horse which on one side was as white as milk and on the other was as red as silk. The saddle-bow was of fine

gold; powerful stones stood in it, and it was fringed with embroidery. The queen was kind and courteous. She turned toward the king and drew a ring from her finger: "Now have this same ring; while it is yours, fear nothing, neither the burning fire nor the water in the sea; and neither iron nor steel will hurt you."

When it comes to the stars tucked in here, the Fine Lady upon her high horse with the sacred ring to secure safe passage between the worlds is a rather vibrant exchange for the constellations Andromeda and Pegasus. Andromeda and Pegasus are usually depicted as a woman in chains and the winged white horse. The lady and her horse wing their way through Autumn skies, sharing the star Alpheratz, bearing the secret of centuries regarding other worlds in their wake, for it was in this region of sky, in the 1920s, that Edwin Hubble discovered the first galaxy other than our own Milky Way, forever expanding our world farther than you could tell me, and twice as far as I could tell you!

Banbury Cross
A GUIDE TO THE STARS

Star Seeker's Key

ANDROMEDA
Fine Lady

PEGASUS
White Horse

EQUULEUS
Foal

The Great Square of Pegasus occupies a rather sparse patch in the star field, and on November nights can be seen nearly overhead when you're facing south. To find Pegasus, begin with the Big Dipper, which is in the north on November nights, with its cup open toward the South. Following a line from the pointers of the Big Dipper through Polaris, keep going twice as far beyond Polaris to Pegasus, which appears as four stars making a great square, imagined as the winged horse's body.

The northernmost star of this square is Alpheratz, a star which Pegasus shares with Andromeda, the Fine Lady of our rhyme, who gallops along through the night with rings on her fingers and bells on her toes. On clear nights, you can take a journey two stars left and two faint stars north from Alpheratz to a tiny smudge of light that is actually the Andromeda galaxy, the furthest object from us on Earth that can be seen with the naked eye.

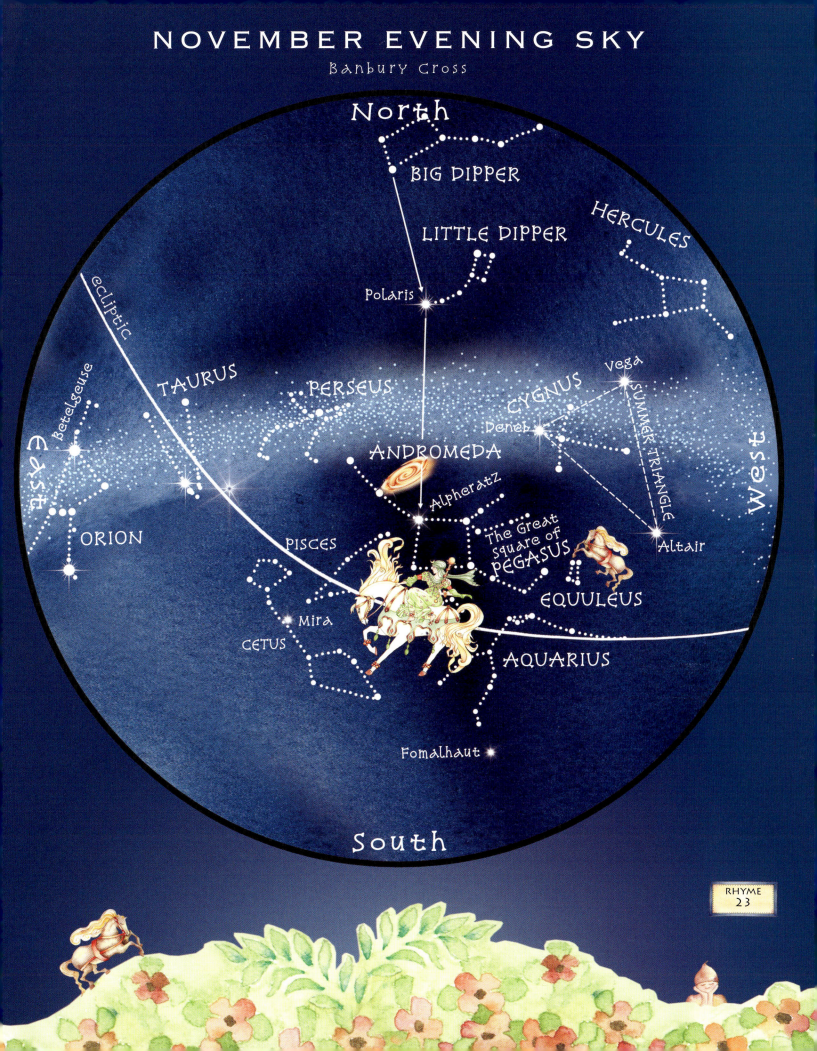

Goosey Goosey Gander
STAR RHYME

Each night when off to sleep
    I bound,
The star goose she twinkles,
    and wraps me 'round.
"Little star sleeper,"
    she whispers to me,
"As we wing through the night,
    o the visions we'll see!"

We sweep up the stairs,
    by planets and stars,
sometimes quite close,
    and other times far,
We gather up dreams
    as we wing through the night,
We join them with stars,
    and that makes them shine bright!
And then with the dawn
    I float back into bed,
The Milky Way visions,
    a dream in my head,
And always I'm happy while
    thinking inside,
of my nighttime travels
    through stars far and wide,
And I carry a star song wherever I go
With a hey! and a ho!
    and a hey nonnie no!

History and Stars
GOOSEY GOOSEY GANDER

The earliest recorded version of the rhyme Goose Goosey Gander appeared in Joseph Ritson's *Gammer Gurton's Garland or Nursery Parnassus* in 1784, and though it appears to have roots in campaigns against Catholic priests in England 200 years earlier, it can also be found written across the sky along the great Milky Way of stars.

It is alleged that in the England of Henry VIII, priests hid out in "priest holes" to escape persecution. If they were discovered, they were forcibly removed, or "thrown down the stairs"!

But Goosey is also our constellation Cygnus, the Swan, which rises up on the Milky Way each year in late spring, and wings across the sky well into December. Her Lady's Chamber is the Milky Way itself, and as she wanders along this trail of stars as though it were her lady's rooms, Goosey-Cygnus mounts with it higher and higher in the night, prophesying light for the universe with every beat of her celestial wings. The set of stairs Goosey goes up and down is our Cassiopeia, hung aloft among the stars every night of the year. Cassiopeia is located along the Milky Way with Cygnus, where she wanders through the sky.

The old man in our rhyme who wouldn't say his prayers is not an itinerant priest, but the constellation Cepheus, who shows up everywhere as a king, except in Goosey's rhyme.

This is the big clue about what's going on here: The stars were regarded as sacred letters by ancient cultures, a gift from Prometheus and the Muses, who discovered the consonants among the fixed stars and the vowels among the wandering stars, our planets. They gifted this celestial alphabet to humanity on the wings of the mighty Swan, Cygnus, whose rhythmic beating of her wings gave rhythm to the letters to inspire poetry first in humanity, and then storytelling. Those who were initiated into this mystery could read the stars and utter the sacred words, because they had achieved the Order of the Swan. It is they who knew the role of Cygnus in gathering the stars in her mighty wings for gifting rhythm into the speaking of human beings; for this was how she prophesied light for the universe – and woe onto those who dared use this gift of speech in ways that did not support others in finding their way to speak in harmony with the stars, for they would be kicked down the stairs.

Goosey Goosey Gander
A GUIDE TO THE STARS

Star Seeker's Key

CYGNUS
Goosey Goosey Gander

THE MILKY WAY
Lady's Chamber

CEPHEUS
The Old Man

CASSIOPEIA
Stairs

Ole Mother Goose doubles as Goosey Gander on December nights, where she appears once again as the constellation Cygnus the swan, only at this time of year, Cygnus is diving headlong into the western horizon. Note that the star picture for this rhyme is overhead from the middle of spring through the early weeks of winter, while Cygnus is in the sky. We chose the December sky map to give a sense of how the constellations and attendant Mother Goose characters move through the sky throughout the year.

As Goosey Cygnus dives beak first into the western horizon, she trails the old man Cepheus behind her, as well as Cassiopeia, the stair set, also on the Milky Way, further east. Note that Cepheus looks rather like a simple line drawing of a house, with the peak of his roof pointing northward, not to be confused with the dragon Draco's head (known as the lozenge) which is north along the horizon from Cygnus.

While you're out hunting for Goosey Gander on December nights, don't miss the season finale of meteor showers: The Geminids which peak overnight December 13–14; and the Ursids, which peak overnight on the winter solstice, December 21st.

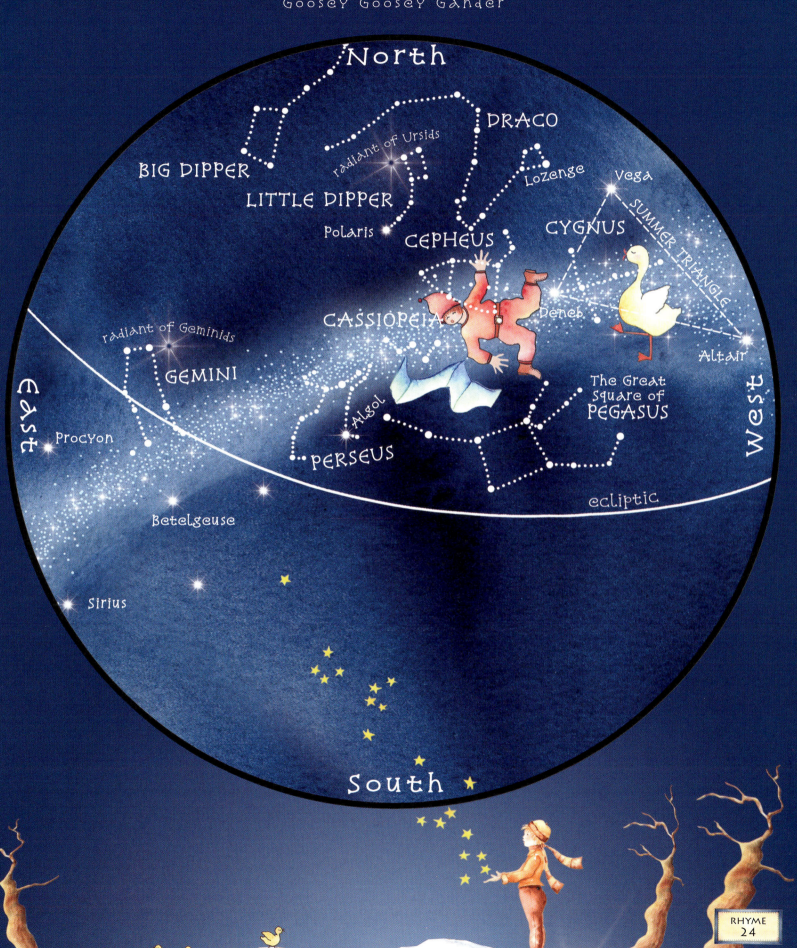

The Star Tales of Mother Goose

Part III

Glossary
Names and Places
Bibliography
Quick Reference Guide

GLOSSARY

Star Names, Constellations, and astronomy references made in the Star Tales of Mother Goose

ANDROMEDA GALAXY
A spiral galaxy in the Andromeda constellation; first galaxy other than our own to be discovered by astronomers.

ARCTURUS
One of the oldest-known named stars in the sky, Arcturus belongs to the constellation Boötes and is one of our favorite stars to use for finding our way through the sky with Mother Goose.

ASTERISM
A group of bright stars that form a pattern. The pattern may appear within a single constellation, like the Big Dipper asterism within Ursa Major; or by joining stars from separate constellations, like the Summer Triangle asterism, which is formed by stars from the constellations Cygnus, Lyra, and Aquila.

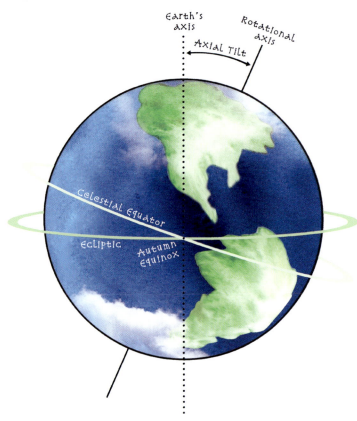

AXIAL TILT
The Earth's axis is a straight line imagined through the center of the Earth that is perpendicular to the plane of the Earth's orbit (ecliptic). You might imagine that this line connects the poles to one another, but it doesn't. This is because the Earth is slightly tilted relative to its plane of orbit—and this is why we experience seasons, or greater daylight followed by greater darkness throughout the cycle of the year. The angle between Earth's axis and its rotational axis is known as the axial tilt. Kind of confusing, so we have Humpty Dumpty to help us out!

BEEHIVE CLUSTER
An open star cluster located at the center of the constellation Cancer, the Crab. This cluster is identified as M44 in Charles Messier's astronomy catalogue, and also has the name Praësepe, which means "manger." This is where the Queen gets her honey in Sixpence.

BIG DIPPER
An asterism in the constellation Ursa Major, made up of seven stars that take the form of a large spoon or ladle. The stars are: Alkaid (tip of Dipper's handle); Mizar (a double star at the bend in the handle); Alioth (fat tail end of the eastern sheep); Megrez (where handle joins cup); Phecda (base of cup, handle side); Merak and Dubhe, known as the "pointers" because they point to the North Star, Polaris.

BOÖTES
Ancient constellation and home to one of the oldest-known named stars, Arcturus. Sometimes referred to as a "bear herder" because he herds the bear constellations around the North Star, Boötes is known in our Mother Goose world as Bo Peep.

GLOSSARY

BOÖTIDS
A weak but beautiful early summer meteor shower that is active from June 26 to July 2 each year, from the parent comet 7P/Pons-Winnecke, and radiating into the night from near the head of Boötes.

CANIS MINOR
The ancient constellation of the Little Dog.

CASSIOPEIA
The ancient constellation of the Queen, wife of Cepheus the King, and the mother of Andromeda, the woman in chains. In our Mother Goose imaginings she is freed from her vain proclamations, and shows up instead eating bread and honey in Sixpence, and as the stair set in Goosey Gander.

CELESTIAL EQUATOR
The great circle on the celestial sphere that is on the same plane as the Earth's equator, allowing us to determine north and south among the stars.

CELESTIAL HEMISPHERES
The two regions of sky that are divided by the celestial equator, and which allow for describing the regions of the sky where constellations appear; these hemispheres are coincident with the northern and southern hemispheres on the Earth.

CELESTIAL SPHERE
The apparent sphere surrounding the Earth in which all the planets and stars appear.

CEPHEUS
An ancient constellation, known as the King. In Ethiopia, Cepheus was regarded as the father of astronomy, and in Mother Goose he shows up in many guises: as the King in Sixpence; as the merry soul King Cole; and as the old man who wouldn't say his prayers in Goosey, Goosey Gander.

CIRCUMPOLAR
Constellations that are in the region of sky near the north or south celestial poles that never set below the horizon; in the northern hemisphere there are five such constellations: the king, his queen, two bears, and a dragon!

48 CLASSICAL CONSTELLATIONS
The number of constellations described in Claudius Ptolemy's Almagest from the 1st century AD.

88 CONSTELLATIONS
The number of constellations currently recognized by the International Astronomer's Union, 40 of which were created during the Middle Ages and afterward. These 40 are not rooted in the ancient belief about the human being's origin among the stars and therefore lack the mythological relationships of the classical constellations. Monoceros in the rhyme of the Lion and the Unicorn is one of these new constellations.

GLOSSARY

COLURE
An imaginary line, technically described as a "principle meridian," drawn from east to west, or north to south, that intersects the North Star. The equinoctial colure is the principle east/west meridian; the solstitial colure is the north/south meridian.

CONSTELLATION
A group of stars that form a pattern in the sky; also, one of 88 regions of the sky defined by the International Astronomers Union, with various shapes and sizes defined by specific boundaries.

CORONA BOREALIS
Also known as the Northern Crown, a constellation of the northern celestial hemisphere battled for by the Lion and the Unicorn, and serving as the starry bowl for ole King Cole.

CORVUS
The constellation of the black bird that rides along the serpent Hydra's back beneath Virgo, the maiden, especially active in the rhyme Sixpence.

CYGNUS
The celestial swan, who takes center stage as our Mother Goose, wings outstretched as she flies along the Milky Way. Her tail star Deneb marks the northern-most point of the asterism of the Summer Triangle.

ECLIPTIC
The apparent path of the Sun, Moon and planets as they move through the sky in the course of the year. The ecliptic passes through the 12 regions of zodiac stars only, so Sun, Moon and planets are only ever seen wandering among these stars. Ophiucus does stick his foot onto this path, so technically there are 13 constellations here, but he's not in any of our rhymes.

EQUINOX
Two points in the year when day and night are of equal length, because the Sun appears to cross over the celestial equator, heading north in the spring, and south in the fall, for the northern hemisphere.

EQUULEUS
The constellation of the little horse or foal, one of the original 48 constellations of Ptolemy, which prances through our Star Tales as one of King Humpty Dumpty's horses.

GALAXY
A galaxy is a community of millions or even billions of stars in which planetary systems such as our own may be found, from the Greek word "gala" for milk, hence the Milky Way galaxy. The first galaxy beyond the Milky Way to be realized by astronomers was the Andromeda galaxy, which is referenced in our Banbury Cross rhyme.

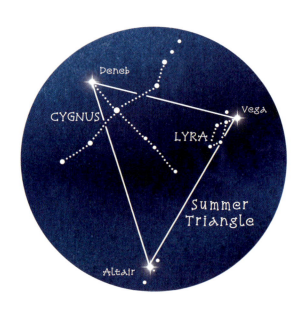

GEMINIDS
The meteor shower that occurs each year around December 14, which has a radiant in the region of the constellation Gemini, the Twins. The shower is attributed to the rock comet 3200 Phaethon.

GLOSSARY

ISOSCELES TRIANGLE
A triangle that has two sides of equal length, which is good to know when you're trying to find the honey pot the Queen is digging into in the Sixpence rhyme. The stars Regulus, Pollux and Procyon form an isosceles triangle around the honey pot, or beehive cluster of stars.

LEO
The constellation of the Lion, with the bright star Regulus at its heart. Leo provides the royal service of helping all Mother Goose stargazers to find their way through the night.

LYRA
The constellation of the lyre in Ancient Greek culture, the stringed harp-like instrument of Apollo. Lyra was also known as the fiddle in medieval Bohemian culture.

M44
The 44th object listed in Charles Messier's 18th century catalogue. M44 is an open star cluster in the region of the constellation Cancer, and is known as the beehive cluster, and as Praësepe, the manger. This is the region where we imagine the Queen gets her honey in Sixpence.

MAUNDER MINIMUM
An unusual period of low sunspot activity from 1645 to 1715 that almost exactly coincided with the reign of the Sun King, Louis XIV in France. There was also a severe cold that swept through Europe at the same time, until Mother Goose came to the rescue.

METEOR SHOWER
What appear to us as beautifully falling stars bearing wishes Earthward are described by science as particles left in the trail of comets that come whizzing through our planetary system. As these particles strike our atmosphere, they burn up, leaving beautiful trails across the sky. Meteor showers are named for the constellation from which they appear to emanate, such as the June Boötids from Boötes, which we like to call the meteors of Bo Peep.

MILKY WAY
The name given to our galaxy, which appears as a beautiful path whereon most of the stars that span our sky are gathered. Because the Earth is moving through space, our orientation to this starry path shifts through the seasons, sometimes affording views of the richest region of Milky Way stars, sometimes not so, as in May, when the Milky Way runs away from our view, as delightfully revealed in the rhyme of Hey Diddle Diddle. Mother Goose, as Cygnus, can also be seen flying along the Milky Way.

MONOCEROS
The faint constellation of the Unicorn, which was created by Petrus Plancius in the 17th century. The unicorn rises up in battle for the crown Corona Borealis in the ditty of the Lion and the Unicorn.

NEW MOON
The phase of Moon each month when it is in the same region of sky as the Sun, and therefore not visible to us on Earth. Since ancient times, new moon, or Neomēniá to the Greeks, marked the beginning of the month and was used to determine the festival celebrations.

NORTH STAR
Polaris, at the tail end of the constellation Ursa Minor, the Little Bear or Little Dipper. This star is important because it never sets below the horizon in the northern hemisphere, standing nearly directly above the north polar axis of the Earth. Polaris is the only star in our sky that seems to not move. In fact, all of the other stars seem to circle around it. But don't be fooled, it's important for showing us the way north, but it's not very bright.

GLOSSARY

PEGASUS
The constellation of the winged horse that looks like a large square among the stars, bearing his fine lady across the sky in the Banbury Cross ditty, and rising up to help out Humpty Dumpty with his fellow horse Equuleus and the King's men.

PERSEUS
The constellation of the hero that strives along the Milky Way in an effort to rescue the Humpty Dumpty Sun from falling through the sky.

POLARIS
See North Star

PRECESSION
The slow shift of the Earth's axis as it rotates and orbits through the stars. Over thousands of years this shift causes our orientation to the stars to change, which explains why the North Star for the Ancient Egyptians was Thuban, in the tail of the Dragon, while in our era, it is Polaris, in the constellation of the Little Bear.

RADIANT
The point among the stars from which meteors seem to fall through the sky. The constellation that is home to the radiant lends its name to the meteor shower, like the Perseids, which radiate from the region of Perseus.

SAGITTA
One of the smallest constellations in the sky, Sagitta means "the arrow" in Latin, and it shows up as the pipe for Old King Cole.

SOLSTICE
Means the "standing still of the Sun" and marks two points in the cycle of the year when the Humpty Dumpty Sun is highest above or furthest below the Celestial Equator. When Sun is highest, we have greatest daylight and this is called summer solstice; when Sun is furthest below, we have greater darkness. This marks the onset of winter.

SPICA
The brightest star in the constellation Virgo; sometimes described as the ear of corn or shaft of wheat. Spica is a bright star on the ecliptic, which is the maid's clothesline in Sixpence.

STAR LORE HISTORIAN
One who is at work restoring the mythic grandeur of knowing the stars by fastening the underpinnings of the celestial empire to the cultural arts of ages, where all the best star knowledge is hidden.

TAURUS
The constellation of the Bull with the fiery star Aldebaran marking the bull's eye and the star cluster of Pleiades at its shoulder. The bull makes an appearance as the cow making mischief several times in our Mother Goose rhymes, jumping over the Moon in Hey Diddle Diddle and tromping through the corn fields while Little Boy Blue is fast asleep.

URSA MAJOR
The constellation of the Big Bear, which boasts one of the most popular asterisms in the sky, the Big Dipper. The Big Dipper stars in the rhyme of Hey Diddle Diddle and shows up in all our star maps, guiding star seekers through the night with its cup, its handle, and its high purpose.

URSA MINOR
The constellation of the Little Bear, also known as the Little Dipper, and as a wandering sheep. The Little Dipper is most notable in our era because it possesses the Pole Star, Polaris.

URSIDS
The meteor shower stream that originates with comet 8P/Tuttle, which peaks beautifully and poetically every year at winter solstice, from the region of the bears, Ursa Major and Ursa Minor.

GLOSSARY

VEGA
The brightest star in the constellation Lyra, which is usually depicted as the handle of the lyre or fiddle, and which marks one point of the Summer Triangle of stars.

VERNAL FULL MOON
The first full moon after the spring equinox, which occurs in the region of Virgo stars; this moon is used in many traditions to determine the dates for the spring festivals of renewal.

VIRGO
The maiden; one of the largest constellations of the zodiac, where we find the beautiful blue-white star Vega. Virgo is the handmaid tending to the laundry in Sixpence.

ZENITH
The point in the sky that is directly over your head when you look up and up and up.

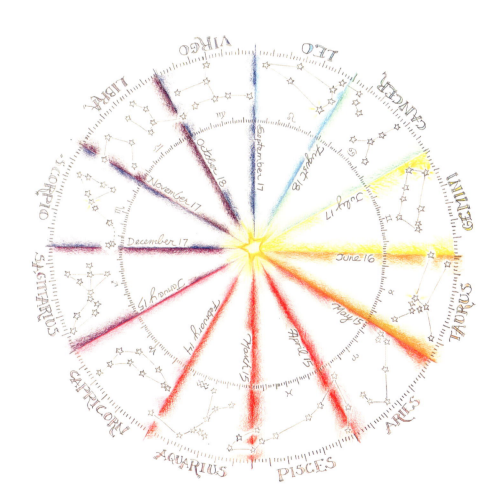

ZODIAC
From the Greek, it means "circle of animals" and refers to the 12 regions of stars through which it appears to us that the Sun, Moon, and planets travel along through our sky.

People Places and Things

Antaeus
The son of Gaia and Poseidon, goddess of Earth and god of Ocean in Greek Mythology. All who sought to pass through the geographic region of Anteaus had to overcome him in a wrestling match. He was invincible so long as he remained in contact with the Earth. Herakles discovered Anteaus' super power, and defeated him by lifting him off the Earth. In our Mother Goose rhyme of Little Boy Blue, Anteaus represents the slumbering hero within every human being, whereas Herakles, who descended from the stars as a son of Zeus, is the awakened, higher nature.

Atlas
Titan god of the Ancient Greek world who holds the pillars of the heavens on his shoulders. Some credit Atlas with working out the science of astronomy in ancient ages.

Banbury Lane
The lane in Oxfordshire, England that lends its name to the cross that stood there once upon a time, and which localizes the Banbury Cross rhyme in our Mother Goose star tales.

Jakob Bartsch (1600-1633)
17th century German astronomer and son-in-law of Johannes Kepler. In 1624 he published a book of star charts that included six new constellations created by Petrus Plancius, among them the elusive Monoceros, our Unicorn.

Thomas Carnan (1737-1788)
The stepson of the English publisher John Newbery, who is known for his children's books. Carnan was the first to publish nursery rhymes under the title *Mother Goose's Melodies*.

Nicolaus Copernicus (1473-1543)
16th century Polish astronomer who set the world in motion with the ideas presented in his manuscript "On the Revolution of the Planets." Though he was not the first to introduce the idea of the Earth in orbit about the Sun, his ideas in 1543 also set the Scientific Revolution in motion.

In The Star Tales of Mother Goose

Entremets
An entertainment dish that means "between servings," made popular in the Middle Ages first as a small dish between meals, but then as elaborate entertainment dishes complete with performers. Just the type of thing to set before the king.

Queen Elizabeth I (1533-1603)
Queen of England from 1533 to 1603. When she died she was succeeded on the throne by the son of Mary, Queen of Scots, James Stuart. This meant that James was simultaneously James VI of Scotland and James I of England. During his reign, the Bible was officially translated into English for the first time.

Floris and Blanchefleur
One of the most popular romantic tales from the Middle Ages, containing elements of the struggle between paganism and Christianity. Floris is able to rescue his beloved Blanchefleur from the Tower of Maidens by defeating the watchman and being snuck into the presence of his beloved in a basket of roses.

Gaia
Greek Goddess of the Earth and mother of the giant Anteaus.

Galileo Galilei (1564-1642)
17th century Italian astronomer credited with being the first person to use a telescope for researching the night sky. He is sometimes considered the father of Observational Astronomy, and when he first saw the moons of Jupiter, he was convinced that not all celestial objects orbit the Earth. In his early 70s he was tried by the Pope's government and found vehemently guilty of heresy, and was thereby forced to live under house arrest until the end of his days.

Henry VIII (1491-1547)
King of England from 1491 to 1547. Henry broke away from the Catholic Church and established the Church of England, which led to his entire kingdom being excommunicated by Pope Clement VII. He had six wives, was the father of Elizabeth I and great uncle to Mary, Queen of Scots.

People Places and Things

Hercules
Son of Zeus and Alcmene, whose older brother Eurystheus was jealous of his notable parentage and so sent him on the famous 12 Labors, including the one in which he must retrieve the golden apples from the garden of the Hesperides. It is after this trial that Hercules encounters the giant Anteaus. Known to the Greeks as Herakles.

Hesperides
The daughters of the Titan god Atlas in ancient Greek Mythology. They are sent by Hera to guard the wedding gift she received from Gaia in her marriage to Zeus, a tree that bore golden fruit. They are accompanied in this task by the dragon Ladon.

Edwin Hubble (1889-1953)
Early 20th century American astronomer whose discovery of the Andromeda galaxy and subsequent contributions to extra-galactic astronomy shaped modern scientific thought regarding our place in space.

James VI&I (1566-1625)
Son of Mary Stuart, Queen of Scots, who succeeded his mother on the throne of Scotland, and his cousin Elizabeth I on the throne of England.

Jean Loret (1600-1665)
Sometimes known as the father of journalism, Jean Loret lived in France during the reign of Louis XIV and wrote a gossip paper "La Muse Historique" about the affairs of court in the form of letters written to his friend, Marie d'Orléans Longueville. The first volume of these letters from 1650 contains the first-known written reference to Mother Goose.

Johannes Kepler (1571-1630)
17th century German astronomer, a key figure in the Scientific Revolution who exhibited a deep understanding of the wisdom of knowing the stars, and who regarded the science of the stars as twofold: "The first is its concern with the movements of the stars—astronomy; the other with the effect of the stars on the sub-lunar world—astrology."

Louis XIV (1638-1715)
Also known as the Sun King, he reigned over France from 1643 to 1715. He commissioned the Paris Observatory, the east-facing wing of the Palais Louvre, and the lanterns that lined the streets throughout Paris.

In The Star Tales of Mother Goose

Mabinogion
Written in the Middle Welsh, these are the earliest prose stories of Britain, first appearing in 12th and 13th centuries, during the age of traveling minstrels.

Mnemosyne
Titan goddess of Memory from the Ancient Greek mythological cycles. She is the mother of the Muses and the first to name all objects in the world.

Muses
Daughters of Mnemosyne and Zeus in Greek mythology, the Muses discovered the letters among the planets and stars, and gifted them to humanity as poetry, the highest of the arts. Their numbers vary, but they are typically regarded as nine sisters, and it is with them that the creation myths began, which is why ancient poets always began their songs with an invitation to the Muses to sing.

Neptune
Equivalent to Poseidon for the Ancient Greeks, he is the Roman god of waters.

Claude and Charles Perrault (1613-1688 and 1628-1703)
Two brothers who worked in the service of King Louis XIV in France during the late 17th and early 18th centuries. Claude, the elder of the two, was an architect, while Charles, the younger, was a man of letters, and the first to write down the *Tales of Mother Goose*. Charles Perrault was a member of the French Academy and is regarded as the father of the literary genre of the fairy tale. The best-known of his tales include "Little Red Riding Hood," "Cinderella," "Puss in Boots," "Sleeping Beauty" and "Bluebeard." Charles Perrault lived and worked nearly 100 years before the Brother's Grimm, who followed his work of gathering folk and fairy tales to sustain their culture.

Petrus Plancius (1552-1622)
A Dutch astronomer who lived from 1552 to 1622, during the great Age of Exploration, when new lands and the stars shining over them were being discovered. He invented many new constellations, only two of which are still recognized: Monoceros and Camelopardalis.

Prometheus
Titan creator god that brought the gift of fire to humanity and was punished by Zeus for

People Places and Things in the Star Tales of Mother Goose

Prometheus cont.
doing so. When he was freed by Hercules, he was able to help that hero secure the golden apples from the garden of the Hesperides. Of him, the English poet George Gordon, Lord Byron wrote: "Thou art a symbol and a sign to mortals of their fate and force; like thee, man is in part divine, a troubled stream from a pure source."

Rhiannon
Her name means "Great Queen" and she is one of the most significant figures in the early prose of Britain, known as the Mabinogi. She was an "otherworld mistress" associated with horses in the mystical passage from one world to the next.

River Cherwell
A tributary of the Thames River that flows through Oxfordshire in England, where the town of Banbury was established.

Robert Samber (1682-1745)
A British writer and translator who lived from 1628 to 1745. He is notable to us because he is credited with the first English translation of the *Mother Goose Fairy Tales* of Charles Perrault.

Rudolf Steiner (1861-1925)
Early 20th century philosopher and spiritual scientist that elaborated the sublime necessity of self knowledge in all branches of human endeavor.

Bibliography

Abrams Planetarium *Sky Calendar* East Lansing, Michigan, Michigan State University

Allen, Richard Hinkley *Star Names, Their Lore and Meaning* 1899, Yale University, reprinted by Dover Classics

Bogard, Paul *The End of Night* 2013, Little, Brown, and Company

Gammer Gurton's Garland or Nursery Parnassus 1783, British Library

Halliwell, James Orchard *The Nursery Rhymes of England* 2012 (reproduction), Nabu Press

International Dark Sky Association *darksky.org,* established 1988, Tucson, Arizona

König, Karl *Swans, Sparrows, Storks, and Doves* 1987, Floris Books

Lang, Andrew *Color Fairy Books* 1889-1913, reprinted 1965, Dover Children's Classics

Opie, Iona and Peter *The Oxford Dictionary of Nursery Rhymes* 1951, London, Oxford University Press

Ottewell, Guy *Albedo to Zodiac An Astronomical Glossary* 1996, Universal Workshop

Roud, Steve *Roud's Folk Index* 1970, Vaughan Williams Memorial Library online resource

Shakespeare, William *King Lear (The Arden Shakespeare)* 1964, Methuen

Tommy Thumb's Pretty Song Book 1744, British Library

Tynan, Katharine *Twenty-One Poems by Katharine Tynan Selected by WB Yeats* (including "The Children of Lir") 1907

Wilson, Emily *The Odyssey Homer* 2017, W.W. Norton & Co.

Wright, Blanche Fisher (illustrator) *The Original Mother Goose* 1992, Running Press Kids

Zipes, Jack (translator) *The Complete Fairy Tales of the Brothers Grimm* 2003, Bantam

Quick and Handy Page Guide

Here is a quick and handy page reference for finding your way from the traditional Mother Goose Rhymes in Part I to the star maps in Part II, and visa versa:

Title	Part I Rhyme page #	Part II Starmap page #
SING A SONG OF SIXPENCE	5	43 April evening sky
THE LION AND THE UNICORN	9	47 April
HEY DIDDLE DIDDLE	10	51 May
LITTLE BO PEEP	12	55 May
LITTLE BOY BLUE	15	59 May
HUMPTY DUMPTY	16	64–65 The whole sky
MOTHER GOOSE	18	69 August
OLD KING COLE	21	73 October
BANBURY CROSS	23	77 November
GOOSEY GOOSEY GANDER	24	81 December

Why are there so many rhymes clustered in one season? We like to think it's because Mother Goose, as the constellation Cygnus, flies along the Milky Way from May through December, and then she dives toward the horizon in the winter months and disappears from view. When her stars are out of sight, that's when we can be feathering our nests with rhymes and tales to charm and delight her when she returns with the spring.

Mary Stewart Adams is a Star Lore Historian, and host of the weekly public radio program and podcast "The Storyteller's Night Sky." Through her research in spiritual science and her education in literary arts, Mary has developed a unique, humanities-based approach to understanding our relationship with the stars. Her work is further augmented by an extensive knowledge of ancient mythologies and fairy tales, which she relates to the research and ideas of contemporary astronomy in order to understand the new star wisdom of astrosophy. Mary has traveled extensively in fulfillment of her mission to safeguard the human imagination by protecting our access to the night sky and its stories, and has received numerous honors for her work. As a global advocate for starry skies, Mary led the team that established the 9th International Dark Sky Park in the world in 2011, which later led to her home state of Michigan protecting 35,000 acres of state land for its natural darkness.

Mary's research in human biography and the stars began in 1981, when, at the propitious destiny moment that occurs in the life of the young adult, she opened her first book of ancient mystery wisdom. The book, which she found on her mom's bedside table, described the cycles of the human life in relation to the harmonious rhythms of the planets. As the youngest sister, Mary longed to be part of the conversation and discourse about the great things of the world that she heard her mom discussing with her older siblings, especially Pat. Here was the key. Opening the book was like discovering the pieces of a living jigsaw puzzle that, arranged according to the principles of freedom, chance or necessity, revealed the endless and harmonious interconnectedness of the human being with the cosmos.

Patricia DeLisa has a unique skill for whimsical art and design that was nourished by the lively enthusiasm of growing up in a large midwestern family, with two sisters, including Mary, and five boisterous brothers. One of her first memories of the freedom of expression that comes through art occurred when she was just six years old, imagining a little being who sat inside her ear and delightfully whispered to her through the drone of the school teacher. Her pencil followed a doodle over and over until the little design lifted off the page into a dancing realization that she could create anything she could dream of: whether it was the nightgowns she saw her mother making, or the rugged creations she imagined the pioneers crafting through stories like "Little House on the Prairie."

Patricia attended art school at the University of Michigan, after which she pursued her dream of living in New York City. Life in New York centered on the fashion industry through an active modeling career, and further schooling in design at the Fashion Institute of Technology, which led to design work on 7th Avenue. In addition to her innovative design and illustration work, Patricia designs a children's wear line under the name Cozy Cocoon.

While we both have many people to thank for the joy and struggle and support we have experienced in the process of bringing this book into the world, the one person that deserves all our love and acknowledgment is our mom, Thelma Marie Gill Hodges. With her gift of creating delightful spaces filled with imagination and song, no matter how hectic a life raising eight children was for her, she was and has always been an inspiration.

For what in poetry and fiction charms,
And yet to our mind incredible appears,
Will with greater pleasure still be heard,
Because it really happened.

~Goethe